Reinsurance: Fundamentals and New Challenges

Third Edition 1995

Edited by Ruth Gastel, CPCU
Vice President, Issues Analysis
Insurance Information Institute

Insurance Information Institute Press

Library of Congress Cataloging-in-Publication Data

Reinsurance: fundamentals and new challenges/edited by Ruth Gastel.
p. cm.
Rev. ed. of: Reinsurance/Ruth Gastel. c1983.
Includes bibliographical references and index.
ISBN 0-932387-43-8
1. Reinsurance. I. Gastel, Ruth. II. Gastel, Ruth.
Reinsurance.
HG8083.G37 1995
368'.0122--dc20 95-10814
CIP

Reinsurance: Fundamentals and New Challenges, Third Edition

The Insurance Information Institute is a primary source for information, analysis and referral on insurance subjects. It disseminates this information in several ways, including through the books of the Insurance Information Institute Press.

Contents

Foreword

Not so long ago, reinsurance was a topic familiar only to practitioners — those in the insurance industry who were directly involved in reinsurance transactions. It was almost unknown in business circles outside the insurance industry.

The public was first introduced to reinsurance in the mid 1980s during what has now become known as the liability insurance crisis. A shortage of reinsurance was widely reported to be one of the factors contributing to the availability problems and high price of various kinds of liability insurance. Today, with the boundaries between financial products increasingly blurred and with catastrophe reinsurance important to the solvency of property insurance companies, reinsurance is a subject of growing interest to anyone involved in public policy issues or financial affairs, from bankers, government officials and legislators to members of the press.

To meet this interest, the Insurance Information Institute is publishing a third and expanded edition of its highly-regarded book on reinsurance. As in earlier editions, the book explains what reinsurance is and how the reinsurance industry functions, from the roles of reinsurance intermediaries and actuaries to Lloyd's of London. Articles written by reinsurance experts discuss insurance regulation, the technical aspects of catastrophe reinsurance and financial reinsurance and some of the challenges now facing the industry.

This book is unique in that it covers a wide spectrum of topics of interest to the general reader and to those in the industry seeking a greater understanding of reinsurance.

The views and conclusions expressed are the opinions of the authors and do not necessarily reflect those of the members, directors or staff of the Insurance Information Institute.

Gordon C. Stewart, President
Insurance Information Institute

Acknowledgments

A book as comprehensive as this could not have been produced without the assistance and dedication of many highly accomplished practitioners, who so generously gave of their time.

Warmest thanks go to the experts who, despite all the other demands placed on them, contributed chapters to this book.

The lineup of all-stars whose views appear in this book includes Gerald Fisher, who provides a unique historical perspective on reinsurance, Bruce Bunner, Joseph Levin, Peter Kamford and Leo Heifetz, who bring a new clarity to the complex workings of the reinsurance industry, and Debra Hall, William Marcoux, Norris Clark and Ramon Calderon, who illuminate key issues in the sometimes arcane world of reinsurance regulation. The Institute is deeply indebted to them.

The Institute is especially grateful to Francis Nutter, president, and James Shamberger, senior vice president, of the Reinsurance Association of America, for their review of the final document.

1 An Introduction to Reinsurance

Reinsurance is a form of insurance for insurance companies — a way of spreading the risk more widely. In many respects, the objective of reinsurance is similar to that of auto and home insurance: to remove some degree of financial uncertainty from the insured party. Just as insurance enables policyholders —drivers, owners of businesses and homeowners — to protect themselves against economic loss and manage their finances more effectively, reinsurance enables insurance companies to plan more effectively for contingencies.

In a reinsurance transaction, one insurance company assumes part of the risk initially assumed by another insurance company. For example, under certain types of reinsurance contracts the primary or direct insurer — the company that writes the homeowners or business insurance policy — transfers ("cedes") to the reinsurer a portion of the risk the primary company accepted in issuing (writing) insurance policies. In return for assuming the risk, the reinsurer receives a premium and agrees to indemnify the ceding company, according to a specific formula, for the cost of losses. This cost may include not only the amounts paid to the policyholder for claims covered by the policy, but also the administrative expense of adjusting the claims. By limiting the liability primary companies assume in issuing policies, reinsurance allows insurers to provide greater amounts of insurance coverage to their policyholders.

Reinsurance contracts for property/casualty coverages may follow the terms of the primary insurance contract, but the original policyholder is not a party to the reinsurance contract. One of the reasons many people are unfamiliar with reinsurance is that the reinsurer generally does not have any direct relationship with, or legal obligation to, the original policyholder. In fact, in most cases, the policyholder is unaware of the existence of the reinsurance contract. Reinsurance does not alter the primary insurer's responsibility to the policyholder. With or without reinsurance, the primary insurer is fully obligated to fulfill the terms of the policy it issued.

Functions of Reinsurance

Reinsurance performs four major, closely interrelated functions:

1. It increases a company's capacity to write policies for higher limits;
2. It helps to stabilize underwriting results;
3. It provides protection against catastrophic losses; and
4. It provides a form of financing by increasing policyholders' surplus, thus allowing an insurer to write a greater number of policies.

Capacity - Individual Risk

The first function of reinsurance has to do with "underwriting capacity" — the maximum amount of insurance a company is able or prepared to write per policy. This is related to the size of the company's policyholders' surplus.[1] Reinsurance increases this capacity.

State solvency regulations generally prohibit an insurer from writing an amount of insurance greater than 10 percent of its policyholder surplus on any one loss exposure, the idea being that a loss greater than that could threaten the company's financial stability. Consequently, without reinsurance or some other mechanism for transferring liability, many companies would be severely restricted in the amount of coverage they could provide. Liability that could be assumed easily by a large insurance company — a policy covering an airline or a hospital, for example — might jeopardize the financial well-being of a smaller operation. This capacity gap between small and large companies is reduced by reinsurance. When large "shock" losses are shared with the reinsurer, companies can write policies for higher limits. The increased capacity enables companies of various sizes to compete in the marketplace on a more equal footing.

Stabilization

Insurance companies may also purchase reinsurance for a second purpose: to stabilize results. (In the insurance industry, fluctuations in profit and loss are hard to avoid because insurance is a service or product that is sold before its actual cost is known.) As mentioned earlier, reinsurance can be used to keep the maximum size of loss on individual policies to a manageable amount. It also can be used to control accumulated losses over a year or over a period of several years. Stated in simple terms, a company decides how much liability it is prepared to assume for any individual policy or the maximum amount of accumulated losses it can afford to sustain over a period of time, and reinsures everything above that limit. The amount of insurance a primary company keeps for itself or "retains" is known as the "net retained liability" or "net retention."

Protection against Catastrophes

Reinsurance also provides protection against catastrophic losses caused by man-made or natural disasters, such as riots, chemical spills or hurricanes. Even with an optimal geographic diversification of policyholders, a company may sustain huge losses from a catastrophic event, although losses sustained by individual policyholders may be relatively small. Without reinsurance, the impact of such catastrophic losses might be greater than the primary company could absorb. How reinsurance is used to mitigate the effects of catastrophes is described in greater detail in Chapter 7 of this book.

Financing

Reinsurance offers a form of financing by reducing the drain on policyholders' surplus, a situation that may occur in a company if premium volume is increasing rapidly. With certain types of reinsurance, the insurer receives a ceding commission from the reinsurer to cover acquisition expenses. This commission increases the policyholders' surplus.[2] The accounting mechanism that creates the need for reinsurance financing is described below.

Under statutory accounting rules designed to assure a company's financial strength, all expenses incurred in acquiring the business, such as insurance agent commissions, must be booked immediately rather than over the life of the insurance policy. In addition, the full amount of the premium must be put into the unearned premium account (reserves) to cover a company's financial obligations to policyholders in the event of a policy cancellation. The premium is only credited to earnings as the policyholder receives insurance protection over the policy period. These accounting requirements essentially put the insurer in the position of having to pay for all selling expenses before there is any revenue.

A company's policyholder surplus serves as a cushion against unexpectedly severe losses. It also serves as working capital for expansion. If an insurance company is writing new policies at a rapid rate, it will have to finance this expansion (i.e., its selling expenses) with its policyholder surplus. The faster the company expands, the greater the drain on its surplus, as this simple example shows.

How Statutory Accounting Rules Drain Capital

Capital:		$600
Premium, one policy issued	$150	
Agent commission at 30%		- 45
		$555
Capital:		$600
Premiums, 10 policies issued	$1,500	
Agent commission at 30%		- 450
		$150

Suppose capital and surplus requirements were relaxed and our company started with $600 in capital. It sold one policy on the first day and immediately had to pay for the agent's commission. It sold nine more the next day and paid the commissions. If it sold more than three the following day, its capital would be wiped out.

This depletion of policyholder surplus creates a problem because the state of an insurer's surplus account is a key measure of its financial health and of its ability to support additional policies. Traditionally, a company might be considered overextended if the ratio of its premiums to surplus was greater than 3:1. Thus, failure to maintain an adequate policyholder surplus can jeopardize future growth.

To lessen the negative effect of prepaid commissions described above, an insurer may decide to bolster its policyholder surplus through some form of financing. One way to raise funds, in effect, is to use reinsurance. Let's say, for example, that without reinsurance, acquisition expenses reduce a company's policyholder surplus by $10 million. If the company cedes 50 percent of its business to a reinsurer, the hit to surplus will be only $5 million. More importantly, as far as the financing function of reinsurance is concerned, by using pro rata reinsurance (a type of reinsurance discussed later) for a block of business, the ceding company receives a commission from the reinsurer as reimbursement for all or part of the primary insurer's expenses including agent commissions and underwriting. This payment reduces the decline in surplus from the payment of acquisition expenses.

Other Benefits from the Use of Reinsurance

Reinsurance also enhances the ability of a primary company to operate its business in other ways. Because it cuts down the maximum size of potential losses to a uniform level, reinsurance enables a company to take better advantage of a mathematical principle known as the "law of large numbers," the cornerstone of insurance. In essence, the law of large numbers states that the more times an event is repeated, or the more units there are in a homogeneous group — automobile miles driven, houses insured in a geographical area and so on — the more predictable the outcome. Thus, the more policies of one type or class a company writes —supermarkets or automobile repair shops, for example — the more accurately it will be able to predict the statistical probability of loss in such businesses, and the closer the premiums will be to the actual cost of servicing this group of policyholders.

In addition, by enabling a company to limit the maximum amount of losses (individually and in the aggregate), reinsurance frees a primary insurer to move into new areas of business, a move that might be dictated not only by the needs of the insurance-buying public but also by the need to improve the mix of business. Diversification, especially geographic diversification, reduces the possibility that policyholders will suffer losses at the same time, a situation that could have a severe destabilizing effect.

But taking on new lines of insurance is fraught with risk. Lacking experience in a particular area, a company may have an inadequate data base from which to calculate proper rates and to establish appropriate underwriting guidelines. In such circumstances, the primary insurer may look to the reinsurer for underwriting assistance, since the reinsurer may have experience in that or a related area.

However, while the risk transfer features and the other benefits of reinsurance can help a company entering a new field initially, it is not a substitute for proper underwriting. The benefits that reinsurance provides have to be weighed against its cost. The reinsurer, like the primary company, accepts a premium in return for assuming liability for losses which may or may not occur. Reinsurers cushion the effects of insurer losses in the bad years but expect to receive an appropriate profit in the good years.

Forms of Reinsurance

Reinsurance, as a business separate from primary insurance, had its beginnings in the 18th century, but it did not become a significant segment of the insurance industry until well into the 20th century. Then, as the insurance industry grew, new uses for reinsurance developed and new forms of reinsurance were created, each tailored to meet a particular need.

Basic Types of Reinsurance— Treaty and Facultative

There are two basic kinds of reinsurance — "treaty" and "facultative." The term treaty reinsurance denotes a type of reinsurance that covers broad groups of policies — all of a company's business or policies of a particular type. Facultative reinsurance covers specific individual risks.

In most treaty agreements, once the terms of the contract have been established, all policies that fall within those terms —both new and existing business in many cases — are covered under the agreement on an on-going basis until the agreement is canceled. Depending on the type of cancellation, some coverage may even be provided for a period of time after cancellation.

With facultative reinsurance, however, the ceding company and the reinsurer must negotiate a specific agreement for each risk covered. This type of reinsurance frequently is used where the value of the property to be reinsured is higher or the operations more unusual or more hazardous than those covered by the reinsurance treaty, and where a careful appraisal of the hazards involved is required. It is called facultative because, in contrast to treaty reinsurance, the reinsurer retains the "faculty" or power to accept or reject all or part of any policy offered to it, and the insurer can choose whether to purchase reinsurance for a particular policy and, if so, when and from whom.

Facultative and treaty reinsurance agreements are classified as "pro rata" (proportional) or "excess-of-loss" (non-proportional) depending on the arrangement by which losses are apportioned. (See Diagram I.) In a pro rata agreement (most commonly applied to property coverages) the primary company retains a predetermined share or amount of the liability assumed under the original contract, keeps

Diagram I:
Types of Reinsurance Agreements

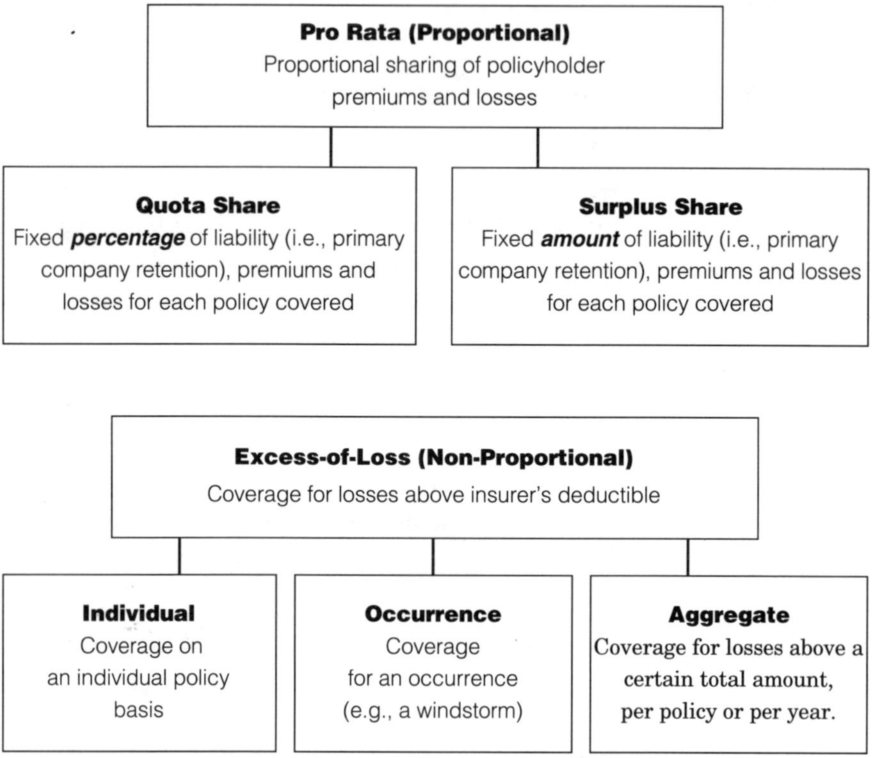

a predetermined share of the policyholder premium, and pays the same share of any losses and expenses. The insurer's exposure to loss therefore is limited by the percentage of the policy or policies it cedes and the size of these policies. In an excess-of-loss agreement there is a "deductible." The primary insurer pays for all loss amounts within the net retention or deductible and the reinsurer for loss amounts in excess or above that level.

Pro Rata Reinsurance Agreements

There are basically two types of pro rata plans: quota share and surplus share. Under a quota-share agreement, the insurer cedes a fixed percentage of each policy written in a certain line or class of business, and receives a commission from the reinsurer for the business ceded. Once the percentage has been decided, the division of premiums and any losses that occur is automatic. In a 65 percent quota-share agreement, for example, the primary insurer retains, or will pay for, 35 percent of any losses and the reinsurer assumes 65 percent of any losses covered by the contract in return for a proportionate amount of the original policyholder premium.

Under a surplus-share agreement, the primary insurer's retention is stated as a dollar amount. If the amount of insurance under a policy is less than the retention, no liability is ceded. If it is greater than the retention, the excess — the remainder of liability up to the liability limits — is reinsured. The premium is shared in the ratio of the retained liability to ceded liability.

Consider a policy with limits of $150,000 and a premium of $1,500, for example. Under a surplus-share agreement with a retention of $25,000, the primary insurer will retain $25,000 and cede $125,000 to the reinsurer. The premium of $1,500 will be shared in proportion to the liabilities,

$$\text{i.e., } \frac{\$125{,}000}{\$\ 25{,}000} = 5{:}1$$

Losses are shared in the same proportion: 5:1. For example, for a loss of $100,000, the primary insurer would pay $16,667 and the reinsurer would pay five times that amount or $83,333.

Diagram II illustrates how quota and surplus-share reinsurance would apply to this transaction. The quota-share example is a 75 percent quota-share agreement in which the primary insurer retains 25 percent and cedes 75 percent to the reinsurer.

Basically, the difference between quota and surplus share is in terms of the retention. Under quota-share the retention is a fixed percentage of each policy and under a surplus-share the retention is a fixed amount. This means that under a quota-share agreement, the percentage of liability stays the same for both parties regardless of the size of the policies covered. But under a surplus share, because the retention is a fixed dollar amount rather than a percentage and the size of policies varies, the reinsurer's percentage of lia-

Diagram II:
Comparison of Quota-Share and Surplus-Share Reinsurance

Insurance Policy	$ 150,000	
	Quota Share	Surplus Share
Retention:	25%	$ 25,000
Amount of Insurance	$ 150,000	
Insurer's share:	$ 37,500	$ 25,000
Reinsurer's share:	$ 112,500	$ 125,000
Total insurance:	$ 150,000	$ 150,000
Amount of Premium	$ 1,500	
Insurer's share:	$ 375	$ 250
Reinsurer's share:	$ 1,125	$ 1,250
Total premium:	$ 1,500	$ 1,500
Amount of Loss	$ 100,000	
Insurer's share:	$ 25,000	$ 16,667
Reinsurer's share:	$ 75,000	$ 83,333
Total losses:	$ 100,000	$ 100,000

bility increases as the policy limits increase.

In addition, in surplus-share reinsurance, the insurer generally has the option to decide how much of each policy is to be ceded, subject to certain conditions that are set out in the agreement. As a result, it may decide to retain more than the minimum retention stated in the treaty. Once the amount of reinsurance protection on a policy has been determined, all transactions flow proportionately.

The conditions set out in a surplus-share agreement usually focus on the size a policy has to be in order to be included in a surplus agreement, or, stated another way, the amount of liability that the ceding company wishes to retain. If the policy limits are greater than the insurer's retention, the "surplus" is ceded to the reinsurer. The limit of a surplus-share agreement or the maximum amount of liability a reinsurer is prepared to assume is normally expressed in terms of "lines." (A line is equal to the ceding company's retention.) So if an agreement is described as a "five-line surplus," for example, the reinsurer will assume coverage up to five times the primary company's retention amount. In some cases, surplus share treaties are layered, with several reinsurers taking a portion of the coverage sought by the primary insurer.

Excess-Of-Loss Reinsurance Agreements

In excess-of-loss or non-proportional plans, the ceding company is indemnified for the portion of a loss that exceeds a specified amount (the ceding company's net retention), subject generally to a fixed limit of reinsurance. In contrast to pro rata plans, the premium paid by the primary company for excess-of-loss reinsurance bears no proportional relationship to the original premium paid by the policyholder. It is a charge based on the potential for loss. Excess-of-loss agreements may cover policies on an individual basis. They also may apply to an occurrence —a tornado, for example — which enables the ceding company to recover losses associated with one catastrophic event in excess of a given total, losses that may involve many different policyholders. In addition, excess-of-loss agreements may be written to cover an aggregate of losses incurred over a period of time, usually a year but sometimes several years. (See Diagram I.) Such contracts often are called "stop-loss" and "excess-of-loss ratio" reinsurance contracts. These and variations of the other basic forms of reinsurance outlined above have been devised to meet specific needs as they arise.

Layering

Excess-of-loss reinsurance can be applied at various levels of liability and in combination with other types of reinsurance, as the following example shows.

Diagram III illustrates how layers of reinsurance might apply to a given policy. In this case, a primary insurer has issued a fire insurance policy on an industrial building to the Consolidated Widget Company. The structure has been built with fire resistive materials, and to fur-

Diagram III:
Reinsurance Program — $20,000,000 Limit of Liability

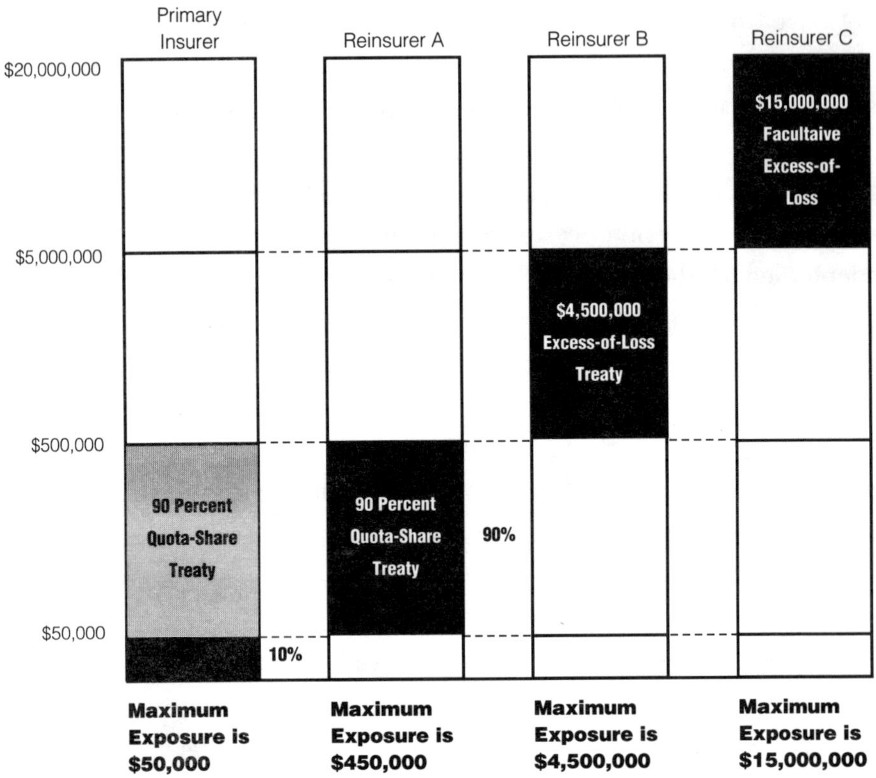

Explanatory Notes:
This explanation of layering has been simplified. In actual practice reinsurance programs may be more complex. Retention levels and the placement of the various layers may be influenced by a number of factors, including the size of the companies involved, the existence of additional reinsurance contracts and pricing considerations.

ther limit potential fire damage, a water sprinkler system and other protective devices have been installed. The primary company's limit of liability for the building is $20 million.

The policy is covered automatically under two of the company's existing reinsurance treaties. The primary company's first layer of reinsurance protection is a 90 percent quota-share treaty with Reinsurer A with a treaty limit of $500,000. Under this agreement the primary insurer's maximum exposure to loss is $50,000, or 10 percent of the treaty limit.

Consequently, if a fire caused $150,000 of damage, losses would be shared between the primary insurer and the reinsurer in proportion to the liability each has assumed under the terms of the treaty. The primary company would pay one-tenth or $15,000 of the loss and Reinsurer A would pay nine-tenths or $135,000.

The second reinsurance treaty is an excess-of-loss treaty with Reinsurer B, which covers losses above $500,000 up to a limit of $5 million. So if fire losses totaled $2 million, the primary insurer would pay $50,000, Reinsurer A would pay $450,000 and Reinsurer B would pay the remaining $1.5 million of loss.

The Consolidated Widget Company's fire insurance policy is for $20 million. The primary insurer therefore needs a third layer of reinsurance to cover the extremely remote possibility that losses would exceed $5 million. It decides to purchase excess-of-loss protection from one of its facultative reinsurers.

Facultative reinsurance coverage is not "automatic" — a separate contract is negotiated for each policy covered. Generally the reinsurer will make a detailed evaluation of the factors that might contribute to losses, in this case, fire losses, and the measures that the primary insured, the widget manufacturer, has taken to control those hazards. Since the Consolidated Widget Company's premises satisfy the reinsurer's underwriting criteria, Reinsurer C agrees to provide excess-of-loss coverage for losses above $5 million to the $20 million limit. In the event of a catastrophic loss that penetrated this last layer of protection, amounts would be apportioned as previously described except that Reinsurer B would pay $4.5 million, the full amount of its liability under the treaty, and Reinsurer C would pay for losses that exceeded $5 million up to the primary policy limit of $20 million.

The above is a hypothetical case. Reinsurance contracts are customized to deal with specific situations so that in real life this program may be modified in a variety of ways.

How the Reinsurance Industry Functions

Reinsurance is available from "professional" reinsurers (companies whose principal or sole business is reinsurance), from the reinsurance departments of primary companies and from various organizations, such as reinsurance pools or syndicates, Lloyd's and government-owned companies.

Pools and syndicates, such as the Workers' Compensation Reinsurance Bureau and the Mutual Atomic Energy Liability Underwriters, are formed by groups of insurers that join together to reinsure each other, sometimes in areas that are extremely specialized or have a high loss potential. These pools offer another advantage. By pooling resources, members of the pool increase their capacity, which enables them to write primary insurance for higher amounts than they could provide individually. Terms governing the apportionment of loss vary. Some organizations require members to assume a certain percentage of every loss. Other arrangements are similar to an excess-of-loss agreement in which members take responsibility for their own losses up to a certain point. Losses exceeding the specified amount are then shared equally by all members of the pool. As an extra layer of protection, reinsurance may be purchased separately to protect the pool itself and to protect member companies for liability they assume as members of the pool.

The Reinsurance Market

A primary insurer may deal directly with a reinsurance company or through a reinsurance intermediary, sometimes called a reinsurance broker. As independent contractors, intermediaries seek out the best available terms for their clients and are free to place business with any reinsurance company that deals with intermediaries, subject to the client's approval. Although intermediaries work on behalf of the ceding company, they are paid a commission by the reinsurers with which they place their clients' reinsurance business. Business is offered to a wide spectrum of the reinsurance market. Each potential reinsurer makes a commitment to accept a certain portion of the business. This amount may be reduced if total commitments exceed the amount to be reinsured. In this way, reinsurance company portfolios are balanced so that large single losses (other than catastrophic losses) have only a limited effect on individual reinsurers. To stabilize results further, reinsured business can be ceded to other reinsurance companies. This procedure is known as retrocession.

Reinsured business also can be exchanged between two companies in equal premium amounts or based on the potential profitability of the business to be exchanged. By trading a portion of its business that is subject to different conditions from the business it receives in return, a company can reduce the probable variation in results. This form of diversification, called reciprocity, is not widely used in the United States but is common in other countries. It is, however, the oldest method of spreading risk and placing reinsurance.

A reinsurance program can be simple, involving just one form of reinsurance contract, such as a quota-share treaty. But where the limits of liability are high, programs may consist of several different types of reinsurance, both facultative and treaty agreements, as well as pro rata and excess, often shared among a number of reinsurers.

Industrywide, the treaty/facultative breakdown of premiums written varies from year to year with market conditions. On average, the ratio is about four (treaty) to one (facultative).

Relationship between Primary Insurer and Reinsurer

Reinsurers operate on the basis of a promise to pay just as primary insurers do. The traditional relationship between the primary insurer and the reinsurer is based on "good faith," a vestige of a less complex era when business deals were consummated with a handshake and backed with little more than a gentleman's reputation. Although reinsurance agreements nowadays are formalized in contracts, the contracts tend to be shorter than those used in other fields. There is no standard contract. Provisions, except those required by state law, reflect the varying needs of each party. Differences of opinion regarding contract interpretation normally are decided by arbitration panels composed of experienced insurance and reinsurance personnel rather than through litigation.

Licensing Requirements

Regulation of the reinsurance industry traditionally has been limited, because it is viewed as a transaction between equals. A professional reinsurer domiciled in the United States must, however, meet statutory licensing requirements similar to those required of a primary company in the state in which it is applying for permission to do business. It also must meet solvency requirements, comply with general insurance laws and file the same annual statements and reports as a primary company. Laws governing some of the more technical aspects of reinsurance differ from state to state.

[1] The policyholders' surplus is roughly equivalent to the net worth of the company, which is defined as assets minus liabilities.

[2] A ceding commission always has an immediate, favorable impact on policyholders' surplus. However, in the long run, if the commission is insufficient to cover all acquisition expenses, future earnings will be unfavorably affected.

2 Reinsurance Marketing

An Overview

In the United States, reinsurance is marketed primarily through two distribution systems — the direct (non-brokerage) market and the brokerage market.

Changes that have taken place in the reinsurance marketplace over the past two decades — the growth of the reinsurance business and the entry of many new reinsurers — have blurred many of the distinctions that formerly existed between the two marketing systems. Consequently, it is difficult to make generalizations about the characteristics and marketing strategies of direct writing reinsurers and intermediaries and the reinsurers that do business in the brokerage market.

As far as buyers of reinsurance (ceding companies) are concerned, decisions about which system to use depend largely on the size of the company and the individual preferences and philosophy of its management.

There are advantages to each method of distribution. The fact that the two systems can exist side-by-side and flourish attests to the strengths that each brings to the reinsurance marketplace.

The Direct Writer

Direct writing reinsurers, or direct writers, operate through their own salaried sales force, known as account executives. They maintain a staff of underwriters, loss control specialists, actuaries, statisticians and others capable of providing all the necessary technical services. The typical account executive has experience in a broad range of insurance company operations, particularly in the field of underwriting. This background, together with the in-house expertise available from the direct writing company, enables the account executive to serve the primary company in many respects as a consultant.

The placement of reinsurance with a direct writer is similar in some ways to the placement process described in "The Role of the Intermediary," the next chapter in this book. The account executive, like the intermediary, is the person who negotiates the terms and conditions of the reinsurance contract and who reviews all communications; who coordinates the activities and services that form part of the reinsurance program, such as the interaction between the two companies' underwriting and claims departments; and who is responsible for steering the two parties on a course that will avoid major problems.

The two distribution systems are not alike in all respects, however. One of the most obvious differences is that in the direct market, the assuming reinsurer and the provider of technical services are the same entity. This means that a primary company looking for assistance in areas such as underwriting, claims handling and taking on new lines of insurance can obtain those services from the same company that is assuming its reinsurance business. In effect, direct writing reinsurers provide "one-stop shopping."

A second difference is that a direct writer's account executives have the full authority of the reinsurer behind them. They can "bind" or commit the company to reinsurance contracts up to specific limits which may vary with the type of primary business and the reinsurance program required, the policy of the individual reinsurer, and the account executives' position with the company. In certain cases, account executives also have authority to settle claims. In addition, they can speak directly for the reinsurer on all matters concerning the reinsurance program.

According to some people in the reinsurance marketing field, there is a difference between an account executive's responsibility for the results of business he or she "produces," or brings into the company, and an intermediary's responsibility for results. While intermediaries depend on good results to maintain continuing relationships with reinsurers, the results of underwriting decisions made by account executives flow to their employers' bottom line. Because account executives are more directly accountable for the profitability of any reinsurance program, they take an active role in the underwriting process, personally approving terms and conditions, making recommendations on retrocessions (the ceding of reinsurance business to other reinsurers) and closely monitoring and evaluating underwriting results throughout the contract year.

The direct market attracts those that need the technical services the direct writing reinsurer can provide, that prefer to have direct contact and a one-on-one relationship with the reinsurer and that want to keep the number of companies they must deal with to a minimum. The direct writer's book of business therefore may include accounts from a wide range of primary companies of varying sizes.

However, because direct writers prefer to handle a ceding company's entire account or a large portion of it, a direct writer's target market generally is the small- to medium-sized primary insurer. The reinsurance needs of large primary companies usually exceed the capacity of any one reinsurer. As a result, large insurers tend to split their business among a number of different reinsurers.

The step-by-step process involved in putting together a reinsurance program is described in the following chapter.

3 The Role of the Intermediary

By Leo T. Heifetz
Formerly Senior Vice President
E. W. Blanch Company

Intermediaries are the brokers in reinsurance transactions. They bring buyer and seller together. Within this framework, the intermediary assumes many roles, at times the inquisitor, the devil's advocate, the diplomat, the referee, the accounting expert, the tax expert, the industry bellwether, the broad shoulder and, every once in a while, the fall guy.

An intermediary's function in the reinsurance transaction process can be divided chronologically into six different parts —contact, survey, conceptualization, authorization, placement and service.

Contact

As in any other business, there are myriad approaches ranging from the cold call to the referral and from the casual to the purely business approach. Generally, by careful study of the prospective company's annual "convention" statements (uniform annual financial statements required by all U.S. insurance jurisdictions, as prescribed by the National Association of Insurance Commissioners), financial material, such as stockholder reports, historical information and resumes, and by careful selection of reference material from these sources, an intermediary can create an opening.

Survey

Having received permission to obtain all the data necessary to make recommendations regarding the company's reinsurance program, the intermediary sets out on a fact-finding mission. At the beginning of such a mission the broker usually outlines the information he or she requires and determines its availability.

The company seldom can supply all of the requested material. An area which is sometimes troublesome is a limits profile. A limits profile is an array of the number of insured properties or operations by size; i.e., how many have limits of $100,000, $500,000 or $1 million, for example? It is important to have these data by number of policyholders and by premiums for each size category to determine what kind of reinsurance program is needed. If the company does not have this information in summary form, the intermediary must perform a sampling, physically examining a representative number of the company's policies (daily reports) to collate the desired data. In addition, the intermediary must determine the amount of time and the number of people needed to complete the sampling — communication of the sampling schedule is important to minimize disruption of the company's normal work routines — and must also establish guidelines for the project workers, which will ensure equal and consistent recording of the data.

The survey becomes the intermediary's learning ground about the company. It enables the intermediary to make recommendations about the reinsurance program, to offer advice about improvements in specific areas of the company's operations and to answer prospective reinsurers' questions about the company. A good survey will encompass the following aspects of the company's operations:

A. Underwriting
B. Rate filings
C. Claims
D. Distribution of business
   1. By line
   2. By territory

3. By limits

E. Expenses

F. Financial data

G. Existing reinsurance

H. Current philosophies

I. Future plans

Some of the above items require explanation. "Rate filings" should include a study of the company's rates by state in relation to those of its leading competitors. "Claims" includes a variety of possible survey areas, including reserve adequacy, case inventory, rate of closings, number of cases by size, losses incurred but not reported (IBNR), and follow-up procedures with adjusters and attorneys. "Current philosophies" could include an analysis of the company's risk-bearing capabilities and, most importantly, management's attitude toward the assumption of risk. In other words, are production and underwriting goals in line with the company's financial position? This aspect may pertain to under- or over-utilization of capital.

At this point, the intermediary should review the National Association of Insurance Commissioners' risk-based capital requirements and the company's capital position. The size and structure of the reinsurance program may need to be changed to bolster its capital position relative to these requirements.

Not so long ago, it was considered acceptable to structure reinsurance programs and promulgate premium rates based solely on a ceding company's historical operations — in other words, looking back in time. Today, intermediaries must review in microscopic detail not only the book or portfolio of policies in force but also, in some cases, what the book's characteristics will be into the future. To cope with the need for more precise information on the potential frequency and severity of loss-producing events and activities, intermediaries have had to expand their staff to provide a variety of complex services, including actuarial services. To obtain this kind of data on potential losses, the actuary conducts a series of studies, which require, among other things, measuring the exposures of individual property and casualty risks, quantifying actual loss experience and adjusting for inflationary trends. In addition, the actuary must attempt to gauge future loss probabilities.

Conceptualization

After having completed the survey, the intermediary is in a position to make recommendations. These recommendations, which may range from a few minor adjustments to a major overhaul of the primary insurer's reinsurance program, should fit in with the company's current and future plans. For example, a company may decide to increase its insurance writings (sales) by entering (becoming licensed to do business in) new states or by filing new "products." It may be necessary to finance new ventures through the use of quota-share reinsurance. This may require a precise timetable, after which an excess-of-loss program may be employed. Often various combinations of basic reinsurance can be used to achieve a cost-effective means of reinsuring and to provide additional catastrophe protection, statement protection (improve the ratio of policyholders' surplus to liabilities, as shown on the annual statement), financial relief and capacity. The importance of this phase cannot be overestimated.

The actuary may be helpful at this stage, too, since it is important for future planning to know the probability of catastrophic windstorms and earthquakes in the geographic area of a cedent's in-force business. Not just a worst case scenario, but the magnitude and number of catastrophes that could have a serious financial impact on the insurer. New modeling techniques give a ceding company better information not only about how much protection it needs to buy, but also about the retention (deductible) it should choose. Having chosen a specific retention, actuaries can then model the impact on the company's financial statement.

Authorization

At this point, assuming the recommendations are acceptable to management, the company gives the intermediary an order or a "broker-of-record letter," which is authorization to pursue the suggested program. In certain instances during the conceptualization phase, the company may authorize the intermediary to approach a few specific reinsurers, usually those which the intermediary has recommended for the purpose of obtaining "lead" quotations.

Placement

The intermediary should determine a placement strategy for the complete "subscription" of the program. In the brokerage market, seldom is 100 percent of a specific reinsurance program underwritten by a single reinsurer. Depending on the size of the company, the number of reinsurance contracts comprising a program can vary from one to dozens. For example, a catastrophe reinsurance program may consist of five layers and there may be a completely different cast of reinsurers on each layer. (See Chapter I for an explanation of layering.) A skillful broker can search out those reinsurers interested in the lower layers and those interested in the higher layers. This flexibility enables the intermediary to obtain for the client company the most cost-effective reinsurance program.

To have some idea of whether a reinsurance contract is placeable and at what price, the intermediary must keep abreast of the direction of the market and know which reinsurers are interested in specific types of business.

The issue of reinsurer security or, more specifically, the reinsurer's ability to pay claims, often many years after the occurrence that gives rise to the claim, has now become a paramount concern among ceding companies. Although the intermediary is not responsible for the financial capability of a reinsurer to pay claims, he or she is duty bound to give the ceding company sufficient financial data to allow it to make an informed decision about the financial stability of the reinsurer it is considering. Since the worldwide marketplace is currently comprised of some 300 reinsurers (counting Lloyd's as one) and because there is an increasing need to have current data, it is important to organize and communicate information in a format that is both understandable and that gives the ceding company a quick glimpse at the reinsurer's financial condition over time. Clearly, if there are some downturns, the ceding company will request more detailed information before making its decision.

In addition to dealing with the intricacies of an ever-changing marketplace, intermediaries must fulfill the requirements of outside agencies, such as certified public accountants and state insurance departments, to which they must furnish complete details of each reinsurer's finances. All this increases the work and skill involved in the placement phase of the reinsurance transaction process.

Service

Having completed the designated program prior to its effective date, the intermediary writes to the ceding company to confirm the terms and provides it with a list of the reinsurers with which business has been placed, along with their percentage participations. Immediately thereafter the intermediary submits a reinsurance contract describing the terms and conditions. The "wording," as the contract is often called, usually is sent to the reinsurers first for approval and execution (permission to carry out the agreed program) and a draft of the wording is also sent to the ceding company. When all reinsurers to a particular contract have signed, it is then submitted to the ceding company for similar action. Finally, fully executed copies are distributed to all parties.

For each contract in place, it is the intermediary's responsibility to obtain all premium and loss accounts from the ceding company and to distribute to each reinsurer copies of each premium transaction. The intermediary endeavors to assure the timeliness of these reports and remittances and makes periodic checks for accuracy. The speed with which individual losses are collected and transmitted is paramount to establishing an aura of good service. This aspect of service is critical.

The service responsibility is also a matter of maintaining communication with the ceding company as to new territories, new products, changes of philosophy, personnel and so on. Sometimes the company may need help with accounting or new data processing techniques or in evaluating claims procedures or the adequacy of claims reserves. In many such instances the intermediary refers the company to a specialty firm; in some cases the intermediary's own staff may provide the answers. Indeed, the intermediary's role over the past decade has expanded significantly to the point where it is expected to provide the highly technical services insurers now need to plan and run their operations.

As we approach the twenty-first century, an ever-broadening vista of electronic communications lies ahead of us. The journey will be exciting with easy access to literally mountains of information. The ceding company and its intermediary will have the ability to track the processing of premium or loss accounts, to review payables and receivables, to obtain current contract loss experience and to simulate the effect on its operating statement of a change in its reinsurance program. Data on various alternatives will be entered into the computer and the results obtained instantaneously.

With the growing opportunities to refine the reinsurance program as new data are obtained, it will be more essential than ever that intermediaries stay close to their clients and to the markets. Only by keeping current with the company's needs and progress along the course it has charted can an intermediary avert potential problems and fine tune or drastically change the reinsurance program to suit the company's ever-changing requirements.

4 Loss Development

By Joseph W. Levin
Senior Vice President and Actuary
Employers Reinsurance Corporation

For most property and casualty insurance companies, both primary insurers and reinsurers, the largest entry on the liabilities side of the balance sheet is for loss and loss expense reserves. Determining what these reserves should be is a function of the company's claims and actuarial departments.

Two major factors in the calculation or valuation process are the time it takes for all details of any given loss to emerge and accounting for "incurred but not reported" (IBNR) insured losses. The difference between the initial estimated amount of reported losses and the estimated amount at a later date, or paid out in final settlement, is known as "loss development." This chapter will discuss loss development from the viewpoint of a reinsurer in terms of:

1. Claims department functions;
2. Actuarial department functions;
3. Reinsurance Association of America Loss Development Study; and
4. A comparison of primary insurer and reinsurer loss development patterns.

Claims Department Function

In both primary insurance and reinsurance companies the primary-functions of a claims department are to reserve judiciously and prudently, to distribute analyses of loss reserves and claims, to issue funds to claimants at a fair settlement cost and to help protect the assets of the insurance entity.

However, there are several important differences between the claims departments of primary companies and those of reinsurers. In a primary company, the claims department handles the administration of all the claims submitted by the company's policyholders in many different lines of the insurance business. Small companies without a claims department generally contract for such services from a professional claims handling organization. In either case, the claims handling process includes payment of claims, the accumulation of statistics and the reporting of such information. The activities in the claims department of a reinsurer are somewhat different. In settling claims, the reinsurer deals with the primary insurer, not the original policyholder. In addition, it does not get involved with all the individual claims processed by the primary company, only with claims of a serious nature or of high value, low frequency. The reinsurer's claims department also is responsible for providing technical support. In legal areas, for example, it may provide information of a general nature about judicial proceedings and the individuals involved, and assistance in the selection of experienced and competent counsel to aid, when necessary, in the investigation and defense of claims.

The claims department in both primary and reinsurance companies usually is responsible for the reporting of claims to the accounting and management areas. The format of such reporting varies by product line and type of contract. One form of reporting is a monthly account that lists individual claims (especially for excess-of-loss reinsurance contracts). Included are data essential for annual statement reporting, such as the accident date, line of business, location, and the amount of payments, expenses and outstanding losses.

Claims under pro rata treaties tend to be reported in summary form, other than for catastrophe claims. Serious claims or catastrophes are generally reported immediately, as prompt action is often needed to provide proper claims control. In such cases, the reinsurer may be able to recover losses on its retrocession contracts. (Retrocession is a transaction through which a reinsurer cedes reinsurance to another reinsurer.)

Many reinsurers require reporting of excess-of-loss claims at a percentage of retention — such as 50 percent. When a primary company has a retention of $100,000, for example, all claims of $50,000 or greater should be reported. This gives the reinsurer, upon audit, the opportunity to consider whether any of these claims is likely to exceed the retention and therefore to involve reinsurance coverages.

It is a common practice among reinsurers to audit a ceding company's claims files. The claims audit is carried out on a periodic basis, usually semiannually or annually, as a cooperative effort between the primary company and its reinsurer. The major objectives of the audit are:

1. To understand the philosophy, procedure, and attitudes of the ceding company's claims department and management;
2. To allow the reinsurer's underwriters to gain insight into the risks being accepted; and
3. To provide assistance in the handling of difficult or unusual cases.

The benefits of such audits accrue to both parties. The audit serves as a check and balance to the ceding company's own claims system and, in addition, it gives the reinsurer the opportunity to help the primary insurer with its reporting procedures and to reduce the need for IBNR reserves.

One of the greatest problems the reinsurer faces is failure on the part of the ceding company to report claims likely to involve the reinsurer. The main cause of this problem, in most cases, is a combination of faulty ceding company claims supervision, underreserving (underestimating the ultimate loss amount), and neglecting basic treaty provisions. In addition, claims sometimes are not reported when injuries are serious but long-term disability appears to be remote.

IBNR reserves for a reinsurer (as opposed to a primary company) may be defined as the sum of (1) a provision for losses that have not been reported by the primary insurer to the reinsurer at a "valuation" point in time, and (2) a provision to adjust those claims that have been reported by the primary company but have been under-reserved (underestimated) because of lack of information or for some other reason. The sum of IBNR and case-basis (reported) reserves appears on the balance sheet of the annual statement under "liabilities for losses and loss adjustment expense."

After the audit has been carried out, the overall results are shared with the primary company's claims manager. The audit's ultimate purpose is to summarize briefly the amount by which reinsured claims cases may be changed, opened or closed.

Perhaps the most important role of the reinsurer's claims department is to establish reserves for losses. The reserving phase can be thought of as the integration of the reporting, investigation, research and underwriting processes. The methods and procedures vary by line and form of coverage. Usually no special attention is given to pro rata reinsurance since the ceded gross loss is used as the basis for the reinsurer's portion of liability.

In calculating reserves, treaty excess-of-loss casualty coverages offer the greatest challenge to claims examiners. There is no set rule for determining correct reserves. In liability cases, the reinsurer will generally follow the reserve practices of the ceding company. However, if in the judgment of the examiner the primary company's reserve is too high or too low, an appropriate adjustment is made.

Actuarial Department Function

The actuary usually determines the amount of IBNR reserves. This is done by a process of estimation, according to historic loss development patterns. Accepted actuarial methods then are applied to trend, adjust or otherwise modify such data so that ultimate loss costs by line and by accident-year-of-business can be estimated.

Reported losses are defined as the sum of the valuation of reported unpaid losses at various points of time and the accumulation of paid claims to that point in time. These data usually are set out in a triangular array (see Exhibit A). Since the main objective of actuaries is to determine ultimate costs of each line of business by accident year, they must necessarily rely on various projection methods, using known data to project the future development path of those data. At any point in time the difference between ultimate loss costs and the reported losses to that point is considered IBNR. (This terminology is usual but somewhat misleading. Differences between reported losses and ultimate loss costs will arise because of incorrect estimation, in addition to non-reported losses.)

It is the actuary's role to carry out studies on these data on a regular basis, either monthly, quarterly or at least annually. The actuary's report on the amount of reserves needed is transmitted to company management and eventually to the company's accounting

Exhibit A:

Reported Losses by Year of Accident

Basic Data Triangle (000 omitted)

Evaluation Point (Measured in Years)

Accident Year	Year 1	Year 2	Year 3	Year 4	Year 5
1990	$42,409	$ 95,542	$176,673	$237,057	$294,677
1991	31,623	92,069	174,755	241,564	
1992	43,950	136,242	243,534		
1993	46,950	139,887			
1994	53,129				

Explanatory Notes:

This table shows estimates of reported losses associated with accidents that occurred in a particular year. These loss estimates change from year to year as more information becomes known. In 1990, for example, losses for accidents occuring in 1990 were estimated to be $42,409,000. The following year (year 2, i.e., 1991) loss estimates for accidents that occurred in 1990 were changed to $95,542,000, a 125 percent increase over the original amount. The substantial difference between these two amounts, and similar year-to-year changes in the so-called "early years" (those immediately following the accident year) are largely due to IBNR losses. Basic data triangles may be established for any number of years.

department for completion of the required statutory or public reports. For some reinsurers the amount of IBNR is greater than reported reserves. This is especially true of companies writing a fairly high proportion of casualty excess-of-loss reinsurance.

Reinsurance Association of America Loss Development Study

Within the several lines of business covered by reinsurance, none are characterized by the slow emergence of claims to a greater degree than casualty excess-of-loss reinsurance. In casualty excess-of-loss reinsurance accidents may be reported to the reinsurer at the time of the loss or many years later. Claims due to exposure to asbestos or other toxic substances are particularly slow to emerge: The symptoms of the negligence that will ultimately lead a person to file a claim may not be apparent for months or years. More time may elapse before the symptoms are properly diagnosed. In addition, in an excess-of-loss agreement, the primary insurer may wait until the retention level is breached before notifying the reinsurer of the claim.

To aid in the understanding and measurement of such emergence, in terms useful for loss reserving, the Reinsurance Association of America (RAA) produces, on a biennial basis, a compilation of loss reserve development patterns. These patterns are compiled for lines of business in which emergence patterns traditionally are slower for reinsurance than for primary coverages. Specifically, the RAA study deals with automobile liability, general liability, workers compensation and medical malpractice. It should be stated that most of this business is written on an excess-of-loss basis.

The purpose of this compilation is to reinforce awareness of loss development patterns among people involved in casualty excess-of-loss reinsurance or high deductible umbrella insurance. (Umbrella insurance is a form of protection against losses in excess of the amount covered by other liability policies.) Acquiring this awareness is the first and most important step toward achieving adequate loss reserve levels.

The RAA study helps measure and define the shape of loss development patterns, sometimes referred to as the "tail." The length of the tail depends on the line of business and in many cases it varies also by company. Loss development patterns or emergence curves have been developed from the RAA compilations using actuarial techniques to project loss development data to ultimate loss costs. The RAA study uses one of the more frequently used projection methods to estimate the values plotted in the accompanying graphs.

Exhibit B shows the emergence curve for automobile liability, general liability (excluding asbestos and environmental liability), medical malpractice and workers compensation. Automobile liability is seen to be the fastest "developing" line of insurance, meaning that it has a relatively shorter tail. At the end of a given accident year, 27 percent of ultimate auto liability claims dollars is expected to be reported to the reinsurer; by the end of the third year this value is expected to climb to 72 percent and by the fifth year more than 84 percent of ultimate claims costs is expected to be reported to the reinsurer.

Medical malpractice is very slow to develop. At the one-, two- or four-year development marks, 4 percent, 21 percent and 42 percent of ultimate costs are expected to be reported. Only 57 percent is expected by the eighth year and development is gradual thereafter.

General liability (excluding asbestos and environmental liability) is also very slow to develop. The first-, second- and fourth-year development values are 7 percent, 19 percent and 40 percent, respectively. At the eighth year about 65 percent of ultimate claims are expected to be reported. The remainder is reported slowly, sometimes over as long a period as two decades.

Since the National Association of Insurance Commissioners did not require separate reporting of medical malpractice until recent years, limited data are available for that line. Due to the relatively short time that these data have been available, it was necessary to extrapolate emergence curves to ultimate levels for this line.

However, in analyzing loss development, other factors must be considered in addition to historical emergence patterns. Until

Exhibit B:

Emergence Patterns by Line of Business

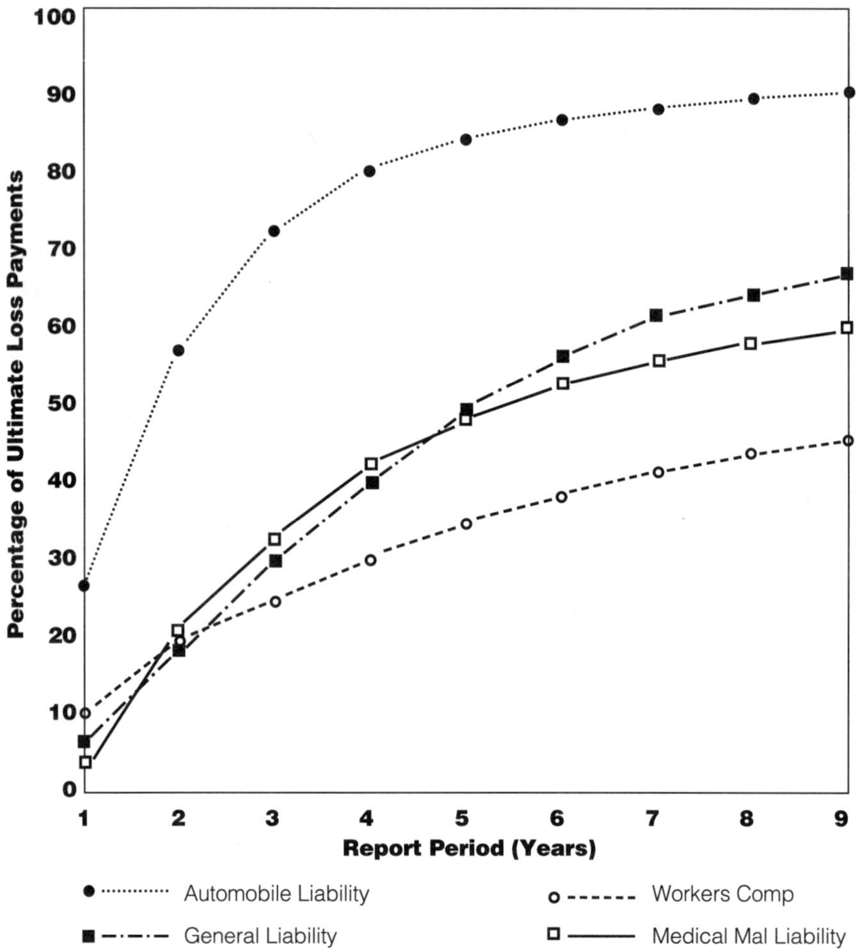

Explanatory Notes:

1. Emergence is defined as the sum of claims outstanding at the end of each report period and the cumulative payments that have been made to the end of that report period.
2. The ratio of emergence to ultimate loss payments is expressed in percentage form and is plotted for each report period shown.
3. The usual range of points is 0% (inception) to 100% (ultimate), a point which is reached after many years or report periods.
4. Source: 1993 Reinsurance Association of America Loss Development Study.

recently, contributing RAA companies had observed a general lengthening of loss development patterns — an elongation of the tail. The current study shows an apparent stabilization of emergence patterns.

To demonstrate this, the RAA compared emergence curves for the four lines, based on the data available at the end of years 1984, 1988 and 1992. These emergence curves were drawn using the same methodology discussed above, but on data available through the year end indicated. An example of the trend for automobile liability can be seen in Exhibit C-1. At the end of the second year of development, the 1984 data suggested that 57 percent of ultimate claims would be reported. The corresponding data for 1988 and 1992 show a different emergence of claim costs — 52 percent and 56 percent, respectively. Similar phenomena can be found for the other lines of business which are shown in Exhibits C-2, C-3 and C-4.

Factors contributing to changing patterns are:

1. In the area of automobile liability, the inflationary effects on settlements of rising costs for the high level of medical benefits provided in some states that have no-fault automobile insurance, changes in guest statutes (laws defining the driver's liability for other non-paying occupants in the event of an accident) and changes in social attitudes.
2. Inflationary effects similar to those shown for automobile liability also can be seen in general liability. These would include "social" inflation and medical expense inflation. Social inflation means increased public awareness of high awards and the propensity to litigate in almost all questionable cases. Changes in the mix of business may also be influencing development patterns since products liability, which has an extremely long tail, is included in general liability. Offsetting these effects may be the yet-to-be-measured impact of tort reform.

Exhibit C-1:

Automobile Liability Emergence Pattern

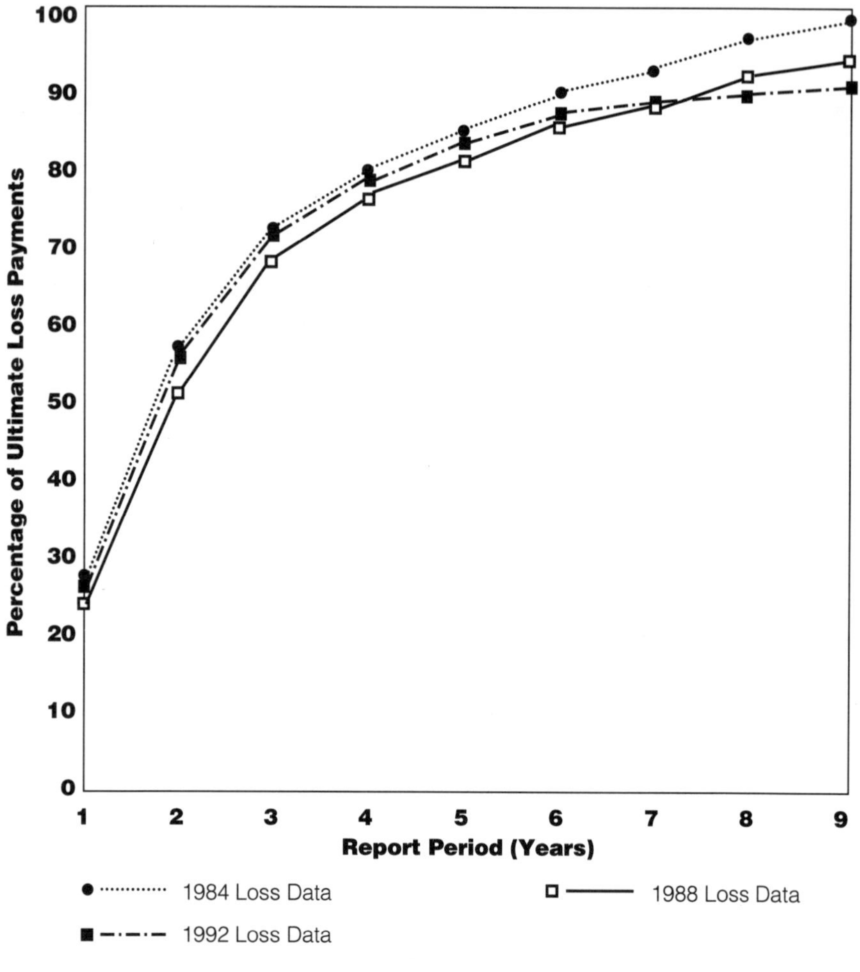

Explanatory Notes:

1. Emergence is defined as the sum of claims outstanding at the end of each report period and the cumulative payments that have been made to the end of that report period.
2. The ratio of emergence to ultimate loss payments is expressed in percentage form and is plotted for each report period shown.
3. The three separate lines are emergence patterns based on data available as of the year ending 1984, 1988 and 1992, respectively.
4. Source: 1993 Reinsurance Association of America Loss Development Study.

Exhibit C-2:

Workers Compensation Emergence Pattern

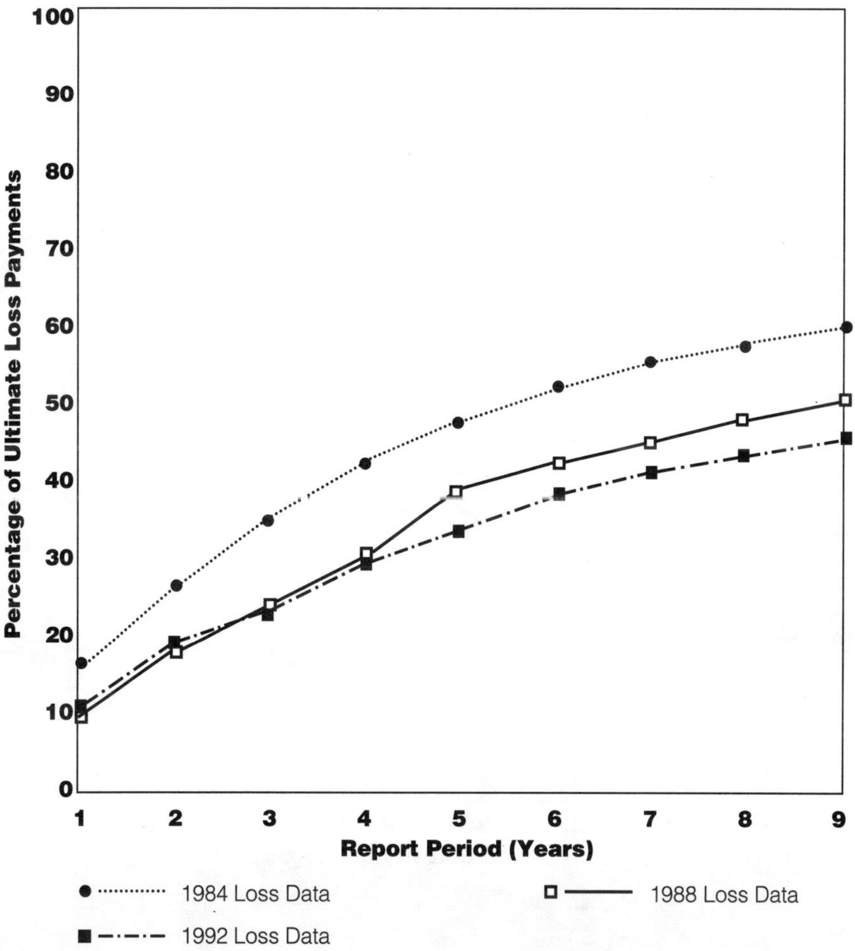

Explanatory Notes:

1. Emergence is defined as the sum of claims outstanding at the end of each report period and the cumulative payments that have been made to the end of that report period.
2. The ratio of emergence to ultimate loss payments is expressed in percentage form and is plotted for each report period shown.
3. The three separate lines are emergence patterns based on data available as of the year ending 1984, 1988 and 1992, respectively.
4. Source: 1993 Reinsurance Association of America Loss Development Study.

Exhibit C-3:

General Liability Emergence Pattern (Excluding Asbestos and Environmental)

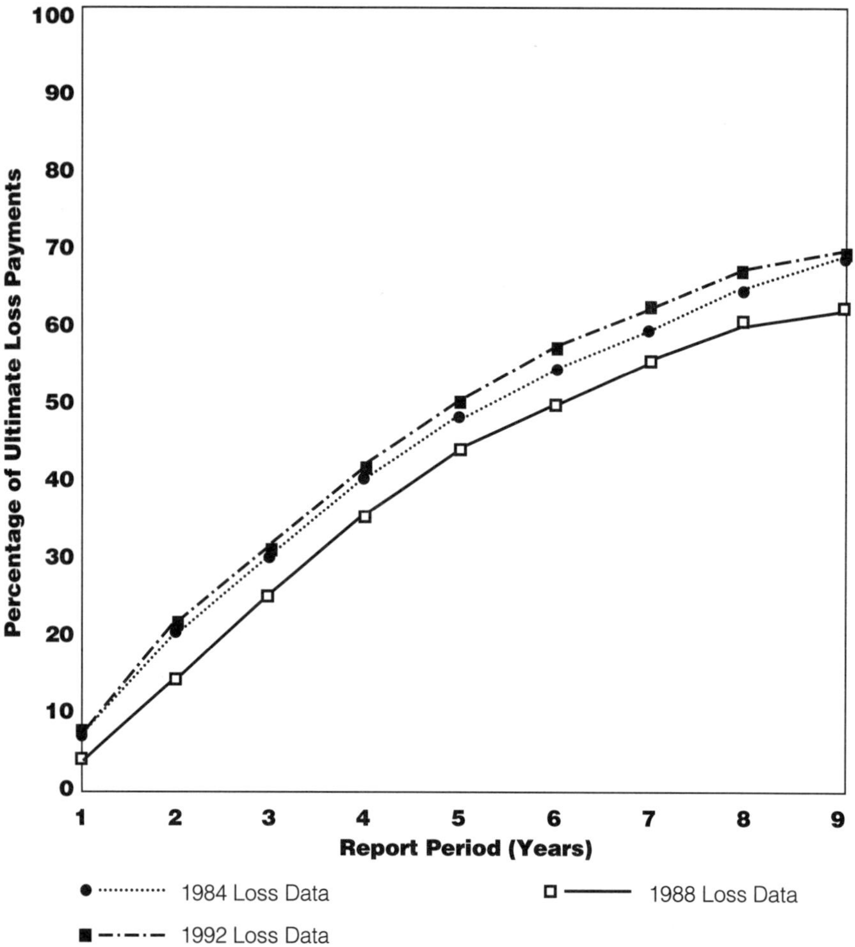

Explanatory Notes:

1. Emergence is defined as the sum of claims outstanding at the end of each report period and the cumulative payments that have been made to the end of that report period.
2. The ratio of emergence to ultimate loss payments is expressed in percentage form and is plotted for each report period shown.
3. The three separate lines are emergence patterns based on data available as of the year ending 1984, 1988 and 1992, respectively.
4. Source: 1993 Reinsurance Association of America Loss Development Study.

Exhibit C-4:

Medical Malpractice Emergence Pattern

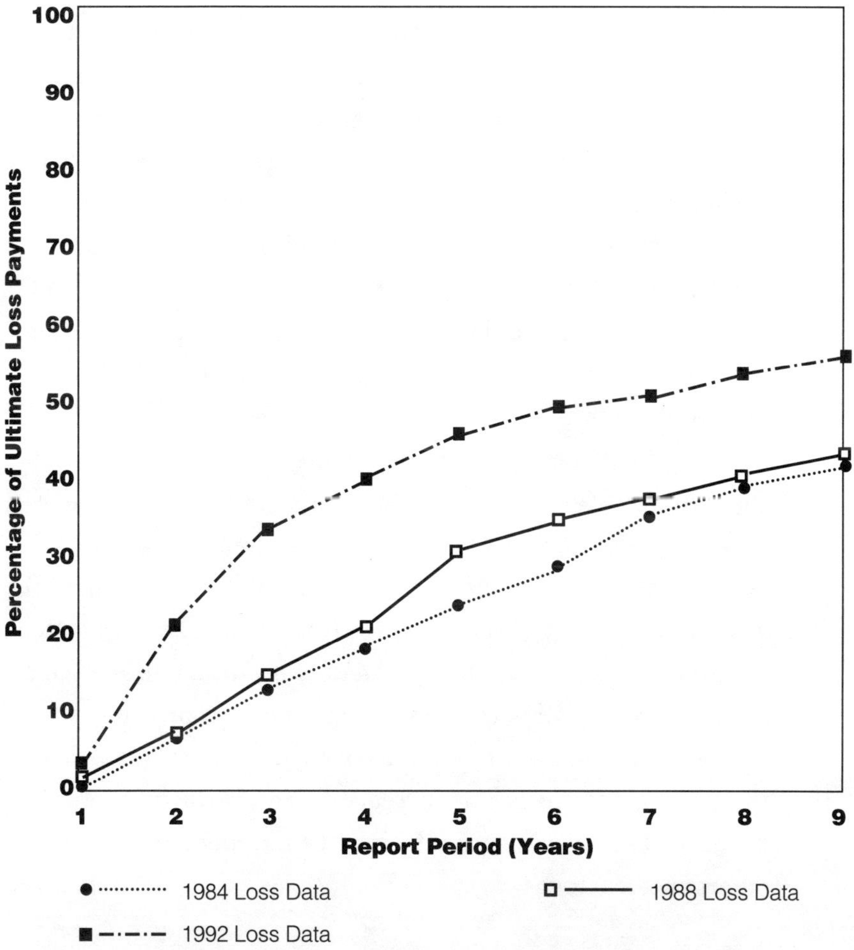

Explanatory Notes:

1. Emergence is defined as the sum of claims outstanding at the end of each report period and the cumulative payments that have been made to the end of that report period.
2. The ratio of emergence to ultimate loss payments is expressed in percentage form and is plotted for each report period shown.
3. The three separate lines are emergence patterns based on data available as of the year ending 1984, 1988 and 1992, respectively.
4. Source: 1993 Reinsurance Association of America Loss Development Study.

3. Loss experience in workers compensation is related both to the cost of medical care and to providing compensation for lost wages. Such compensation would include periodic pension-type payments for long-term disabilities or, in the case of death, payments to a survivor. Affecting development in this line is the increasing emergence of occupational disease claims (primarily those related to the use of asbestos), higher medical costs, increased longevity and a reduced rate of survivor remarriage (survivor benefits in most states are eliminated upon remarriage). In addition, loss development patterns have been affected by a liberalization trend on the part of authorities administering the workers compensation laws and benefits.
4. In the area of medical malpractice, slow emergence is tied to the manifestation of symptoms. For example, in the case of newborn infants, lack of oxygen during the first minutes of delivery may not become apparent until measurable mental retardation can be observed years later. An additional factor pushing up costs is the high level of expectation applied to a science that is still not capable of producing completely predictable results. Failure to achieve expected results leads to the filing of lawsuits. The increased size of awards, including punitive damages, also is a factor in changing development or emergence patterns.

This list of contributing factors, while not exhaustive, does provide a partial explanation of the trends observed. The trends of the 1970s and 1980s are now obvious, but only with the benefit of hindsight. The implications for the 1990s are still uncertain. Reserving for latent injury cases, particularly asbestos-related diseases and black lung diseases, will continue to be challenging.

Since the data in the RAA study were obtained from a diverse industry, the study comes with caveats, including the following:

1. The data consist of losses in excess of underlying retentions. Such retentions vary from company to company and over time. Ideally, excess-of-loss experience would be studied separately for various retention/limit combinations or ranges thereof. The current RAA compilations now address this classification.
2. Most companies are reporting net of their reinsurance or retrocession. Retrocession retentions have also been increasing over time and will vary from reinsurer to reinsurer.
3. Geographic marketing and legal jurisdictions vary widely.
4. Underwriting rules vary from company to company.
5. Loss development patterns consist of actual late reporting, and adjustment of known reserves for incorrect initial estimates (underestimates). For reinsurers, the greatest portion of loss development comes from true late reporting.
6. Alternate coverage techniques, such as indexing, can cause distortions in developments. Indexing is a concept, which, in theory, spreads the cost of inflation equitably between the primary company and the reinsurer. This is accomplished by application of an index factor to the retention of the primary company. This retention will rise as the selected index rises. The effect of this, however, is that reinsurer involvement is deferred to higher levels of coverage but it also may leverage the reinsurer's involvement. This leverage effect is discussed later in this chapter.

If the RAA loss development data are to be used to project ultimate losses for an individual company, especially in the earlier years of development, extreme caution should be exercised. Variance in "immature" years is large. Early reported data can be volatile and lead to incorrect conclusions if heavily relied upon. The RAA study discusses individual company loss development variations.

In summary, the RAA study, which is based on the only known

compilation of casualty excess-of-loss reinsurance loss reserve development data, is intended to make the reader aware of loss development patterns and their variations by line of business. Although accompanied by necessary caveats, the study can and should be used in individual company loss reserve analysis as a guide to average expected emergence of losses. Loss reserve adequacy, as mentioned before, is the primary objective of most insurance company actuaries and their management. Generally, in measuring loss reserve adequacy, it is up to loss reserve specialists in each company to differentiate between their company's loss reserve characteristics and those of the industry average.

Comparison of Primary and Reinsurance Loss Development Patterns

In the prior section, loss development patterns were compared by line of business. The comparisons showed how loss development patterns vary from one line of business to another. They also vary substantially between the two segments of the insurance industry — reinsurers and primary insurers. The major reason for this difference is the delay in reporting claims to reinsurers, despite steps taken to accelerate such reporting. The problem of delay is observed most in excess-of-loss reinsurance for casualty business.

The four graphs in Exhibits D, E, F and G show the relative emergence patterns for primary companies and reinsurers. Emergence means cumulative paid and unpaid reserves at various points in time of development. Emergence does not include IBNR losses. The four graphs shown represent the typical patterns of emergence of claims for a primary company and a reinsurer for automobile liability, workers compensation, general liability (excluding asbestos and environmental liability), and medical malpractice. The plots are incurred losses (exclusive of estimates of IBNR) as a percentage of ultimate liability at annual valuation dates. In the case of automobile liability, at the end of an accident year the primary insurer is aware of about 70 percent of its ultimate liability whereas the rein-

Exhibit D:

Automobile Liability Emergence Pattern

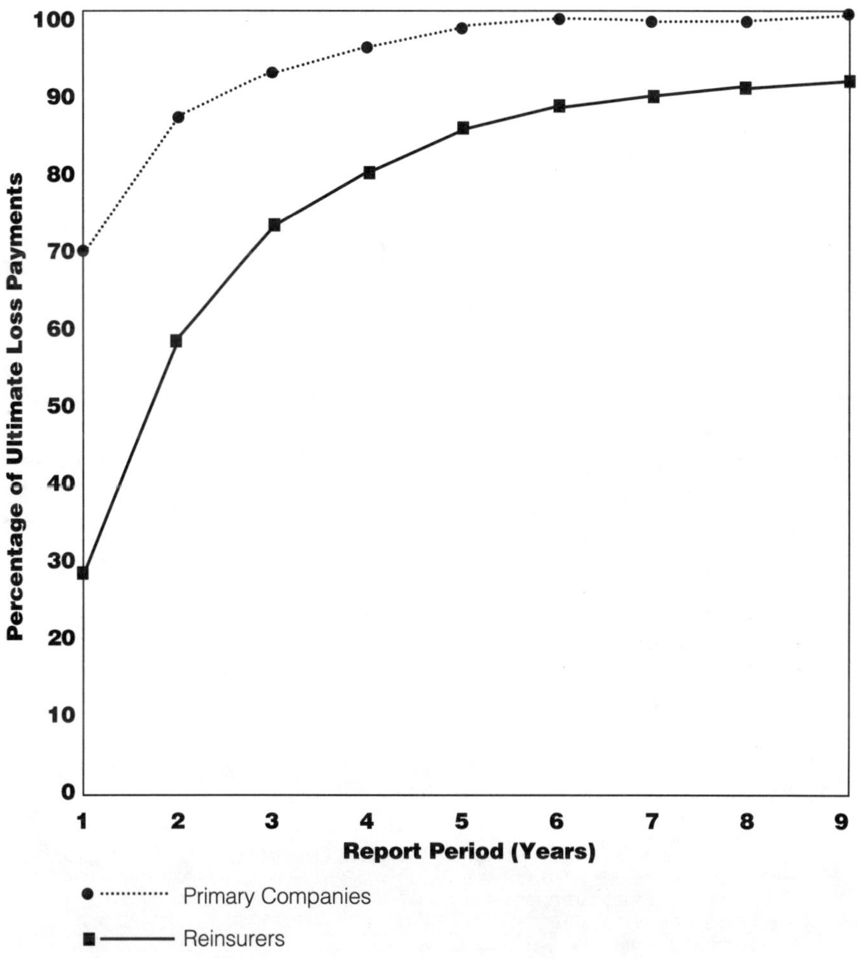

Explanatory Notes:

1. Emergence is defined as the sum of claims outstanding at the end of each report period and the cumulative payments that have been made to the end of that report period.
2. The ratio of emergence to ultimate loss payments is expressed in percentage form and is plotted for each report period shown.
3. Sources: (a) 1993 Reinsurance Association of America Loss Development Study.
   (b) Annual statements of selected primary insurance companies.

Exhibit E:

Workers Compensation Emergence Pattern

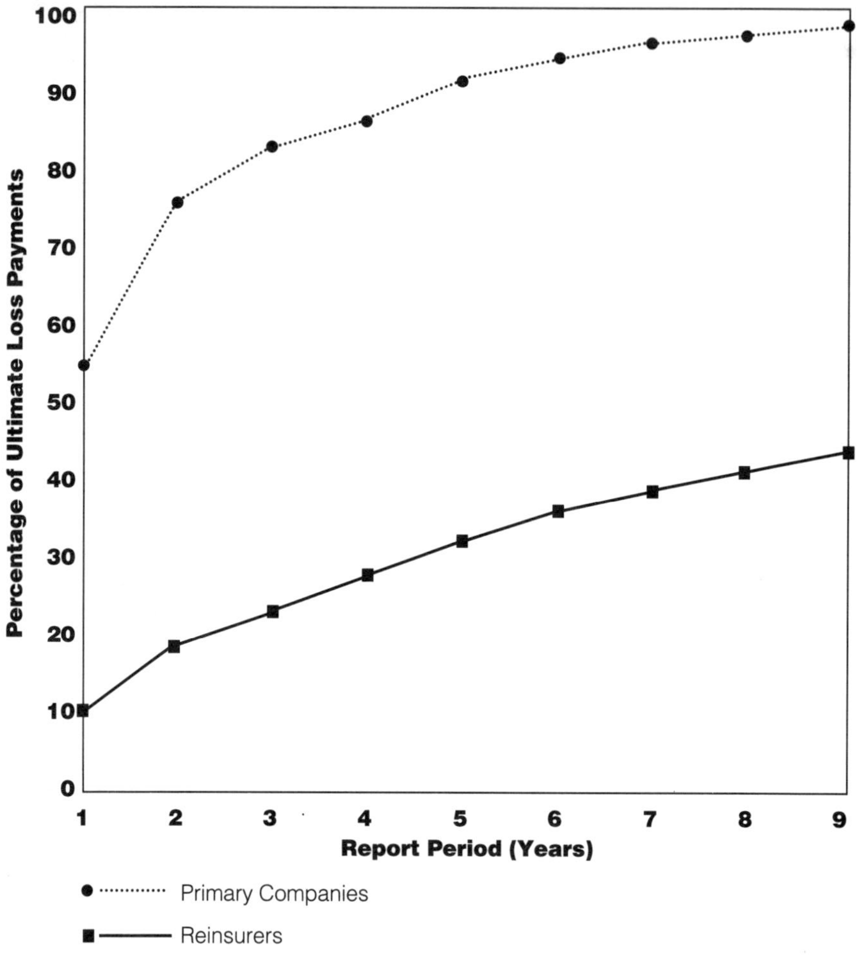

Explanatory Notes:

1. Emergence is defined as the sum of claims outstanding at the end of each report period and the cumulative payments that have been made to the end of that report period.
2. The ratio of emergence to ultimate loss payments is expressed in percentage form and is plotted for each report period shown.
3. Sources: (a) 1993 Reinsurance Association of America Loss Development Study.
   (b) Annual statements of selected primary insurance companies.

Exhibit F:

General Liability Emergence Pattern (Including Asbestos and Environmental)

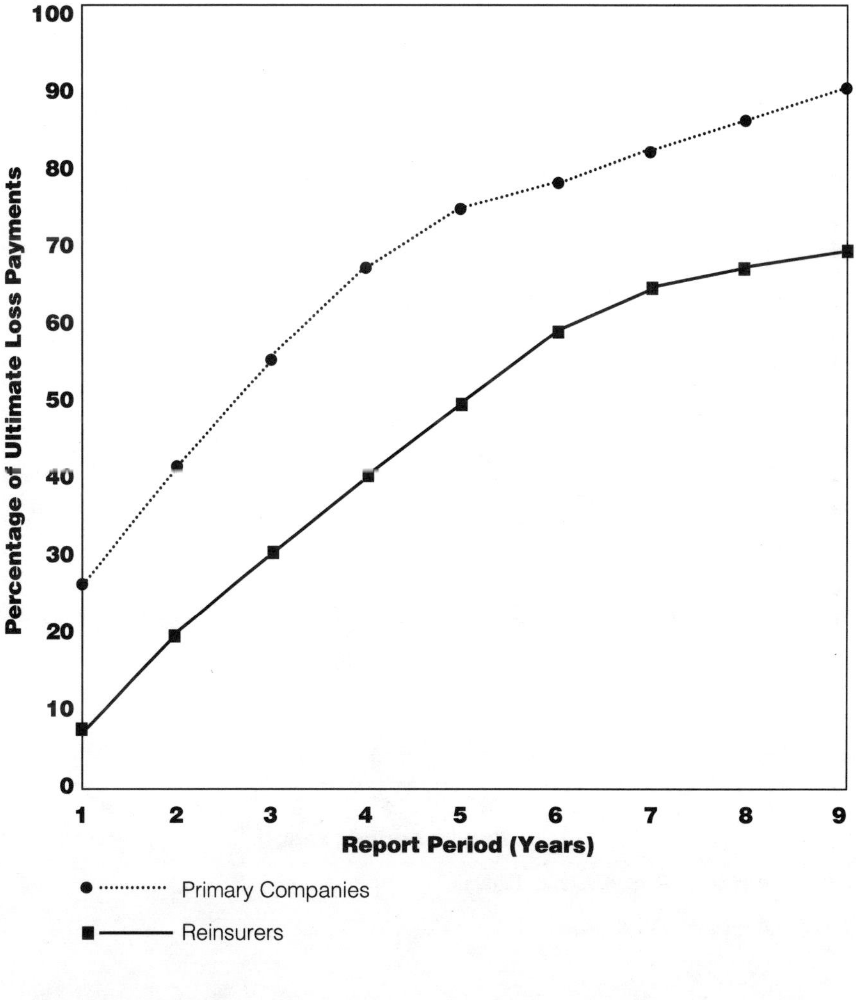

Explanatory Notes:

1. Emergence is defined as the sum of claims outstanding at the end of each report period and the cumulative payments that have been made to the end of that report period.
2. The ratio of emergence to ultimate loss payments is expressed in percentage form and is plotted for each report period shown.
3. Sources: (a) 1993 Reinsurance Association of America Loss Development Study.
   (b) Annual statements of selected primary insurance companies.

Exhibit G:

Medical Malpractice Emergence Pattern

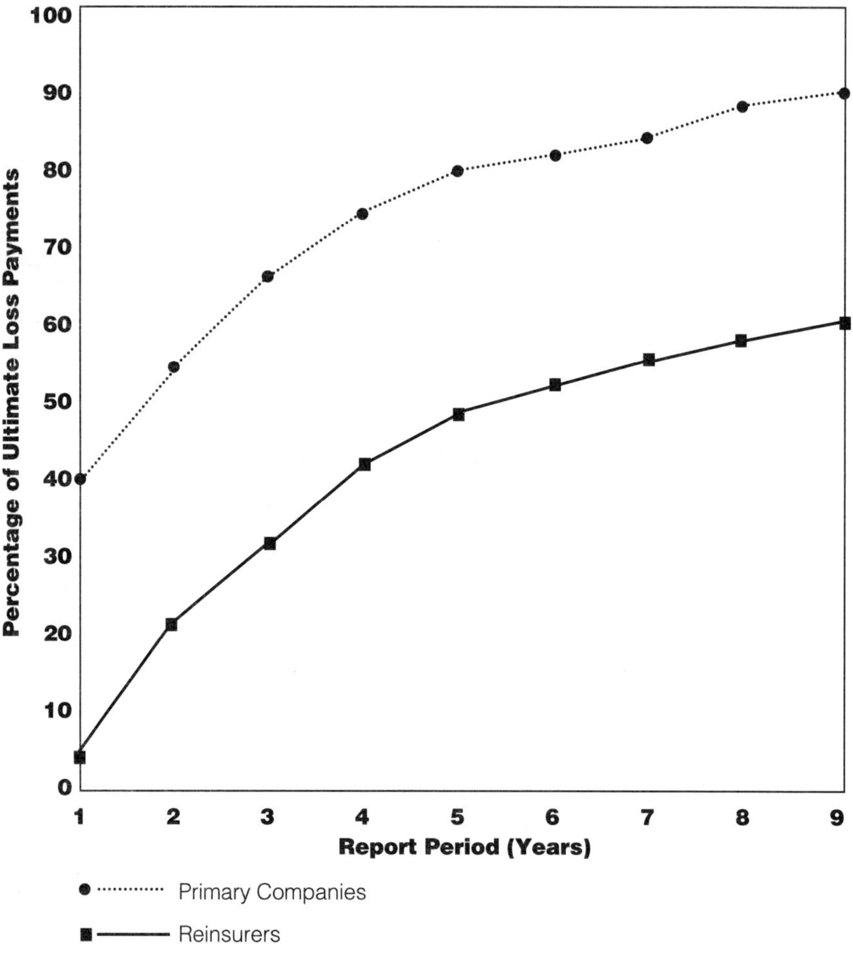

Explanatory Notes:

1. Emergence is defined as the sum of claims outstanding at the end of each report period and the cumulative payments that have been made to the end of that report period.
2. The ratio of emergence to ultimate loss payments is expressed in percentage form and is plotted for each report period shown.
3. Sources: (a) 1993 Reinsurance Association of America Loss Development Study.
   (b) Annual statements of selected primary insurance companies.

surer knows of only 27 percent of its liability. At the end of three years the primary insurer knows of approximately 94 percent, but the reinsurer knows of only 72 percent.

In the general liability line of insurance the disparity is more pronounced. The corresponding data for one- and three-year development patterns are 24 percent for the primary insurer versus 7 percent for the reinsurer for the first year, and 55 percent versus 31 percent for the third year of development. At the end of seven years the reinsurer usually knows of only 62 percent of its ultimate liability.

Workers compensation shows a pattern similar to general liability. The primary company learns of most of its ultimate liability within three years while after 10 years only 46 percent of reinsurers' ultimate loss amounts are reported.

Inflation, to a certain degree, is a factor in the elongation of the emergence pattern. Mention was made earlier of the leverage effect of inflation in excess-of-loss reinsurance. The following example highlights the effect of inflation on the reinsurer in excess-of-loss casualty contracts. Assume a contract has a $50,000 retention per individual policy and that, without inflation, 36 claims are incurred by the primary company, as follows:

The Effect of Inflation on Excess-of-Loss Contracts

Diagram I:

# of Claims Ceded	Amount of Each Loss	Total Loss Amount	Amount of Loss Retained	Amount of Loss
11	$ 15,000	$ 165,000	$ 165,000	$ 0
9	25,000	225,000	225,000	0
7	35,000	245,000	245,000	0
5	48,000	240,000	240,000	0
3	55,000	165,000	150,000	15,000
1	65,000	65,000	50,000	15,000
36		$1,105,000	$1,075,000	$30,000

Now assume a 10 percent rate of inflation overall. The distribution of losses would then be as follows:

Diagram II:

# of Claims Ceded	Amount of Each Loss	Total Loss Amount	Amount of Loss Retained	Amount of Loss
11	$ 16,500	$ 181,500	$ 181,500	$ 0
9	27,500	247,500	247,500	0
7	38,500	269,500	269,500	0
5	52,800	264,000	250,000	14,000
3	60,500	181,500	150,000	31,500
1	71,500	71,500	50,000	21,500
36		$1,215,500	$1,148,500	$67,000

Without inflation (Diagram I) four claims totaling $30,000 were ceded to the reinsurer. With inflation (Diagram II) nine claims totaling $67,000 were ceded. The impact of a 10 percent inflation factor caused the amount of each loss to increase. For example, the five claims of $48,000 each (Diagram I) increased to $52,800 (Diagram II) or $2,800 above the retention of $50,000 per policy, bringing the amount ceded to the reinsurer to $14,000. As a result, the primary company's total amount of retained losses increased by 7 percent from $1,075,000 to $1,148,500, but the reinsurer's portion of losses increased by 123 percent from $30,000 to $67,000. Not only are more claims involved but the average amount of claims increased more dramatically for reinsurers.

Also included in the 1993 edition of the RAA Loss Development Study are comparisons of treaty and facultative business and data for loss development triangles sorted by ranges of underlying retention.

Facultative business was shown to have a shorter tail than treaty for automobile, a longer tail than treaty for general liability (excluding asbestos and environmental), and a comparable tail for workers compensation. Emergence for facultative is slower than treaty in the first seven years and faster in subsequent years for medical malpractice.

The study also demonstrated differences in emergence patterns at different retention ranges.

5 The Lloyd's of London Marketplace

By Ruth Gastel
Vice President-Issues Analysis
Insurance Information Institute

For most people, the name "Lloyd's of London" immediately conjures up a place where people put their personal wealth on the line to insure shipping and exotic risks. Lloyd's is a household name, a venerable institution, the world's oldest and most successful insurance exchange where some of the largest and most complex and sophisticated insurance and reinsurance transactions take place, particularly those involving transportation and catastrophe coverages.

How Lloyd's Coffeehouse Became Lloyd's Society

Lloyd's dates back to the seventeenth century. There were no insurance companies at that time. Following a custom of risk-sharing thought to have originated in Italy in the 1500s, shipping merchants in England pooled the risk of an unsuccessful voyage among themselves, sharing the loss if a pool member's ship or cargo was lost at sea.

Insurance could also be obtained from individuals, people who wanted to invest the assets they had accumulated through other businesses and trade. For a fee, these entrepreneurs would guarantee the financial success of a voyage. Generally, the ship returned and they would keep what they had been paid. On the few occasions that a ship fell victim to bad weather, pirates or mutiny, they paid the shipowner's losses.

Like most investors, before they would commit any money, these businessmen wanted to know the risk of loss. So a shipowner seeking insurance would write down on a slip of paper a description of the ship and its cargo, its route and final destination. A line was drawn underneath this description. Those that decided to accept a portion of the risk would note the percentage on the slip underneath the line and write their initials under it — hence the term "underwriter."

Along with each investor's signature appeared the words, "each for his part and not one for another," to denote the individual nature of the investor's liability. Each investor was acting for himself. If the voyage was successful, there were no claims and each investor's assets grew in proportion to the total premium paid and the share each had taken of the risk of loss. If the ship went down, each would be liable for replacing the ship and possibly its cargo in proportion to the risk he had assumed.

Because each individual investor/underwriter accepted only a fraction of the total risk, the shipowner would have to go from entrepreneur to entrepreneur until he had secured underwriters for 100 percent of what he needed. The task of finding underwriters to subscribe to a venture was made easier when a group of them could be found in one place. That place was Lloyd's.

Lloyd's began in 1688 as a coffeehouse. Coffee was expensive and fashionable in seventeenth century London and rich merchants used to meet at Lloyd's to drink their morning coffee.

Nobody knows exactly when the first insurance transaction took place but it's not hard to imagine a group of businessmen sitting around a table, exchanging the latest news — whose ship was overdue, what they stood to lose if it failed to return, who had heard what. It suddenly occurs to one shipowner that it would be easier to ask his friends around the table to share the risk of his next voyage, and finalize the transaction right there in the coffeehouse, than to make the rounds of all the investors scattered throughout the city. His friends immediately saw this as an opportunity to make money without much effort and agreed to the proposal. Before long, the initial circle of investors had broadened to include other business acquaintances and soon the coffeehouse became known as a place where wealthy merchants willing to underwrite shipping ventures congregated.

Lloyd's coffeehouse quickly became the principal center for the transaction of marine insurance and the gathering of marine intelligence. Here, people who wanted inside information on shipping could meet those in a position to give it. Since insurance might be taken out only when a shipowner feared the vessel was lost, it was important to know which ships had been sighted and where, and which were overdue.

Lloyd's flourished but the shipowners no longer went there themselves. Like people who buy insurance nowadays, they found that their time could be better spent by hiring middlemen or "brokers" to go to the coffeehouse for them. The brokers found the underwriters, placed the insurance and, if a claim was made, collected from each underwriter the sums due.

Likewise, the rich merchants found it to their advantage to appoint one of their group to represent them — probably the one most adept at ferreting out information about what was happening at sea. Each merchant agreed for a fee to take a fixed percentage of whatever risks his group's representative underwrote. By joining together in a group, individual investors spread the risk of loss and also provided a larger pool of money to support underwriting. These groups were the forerunners of what are now known as syndicates.

Lloyd's continued in much the same way until 1771 when the underwriters who used Lloyd's formed a committee to run the organization. In 1774, the committee acquired an underwriting room in the Royal Exchange in the City of London, retaining the services of the coffeehouse proprietors as managers.

Lloyd's thus became a club where insurance might be bought from the underwriters that belonged to it. The committee of Lloyd's provided the premises and the marine intelligence for the use of the underwriters but took no corporate responsibility for the underwriters or for the insurance they wrote, practices that continue to this day.

With the enactment of the Lloyd's Act in 1871, the club was incorporated and became the Society or Corporation of Lloyd's. The act also provided for an elected committee of members with power to manage the Society's affairs.

As Lloyd's expanded, so did its ability to collect vital information on shipping activities. By the early 1900s, Lloyd's had set up a series of signal stations, reaching from England to the Suez Canal, and a network of Lloyd's agents around the world. And its reputation for integrity spread far beyond the United Kingdom. When other insurance companies went bankrupt or reneged on their contracts of insurance after the great San Francisco earthquake in 1906, Lloyd's honored its promise to pay over and beyond its obligations. The chairman of Lloyd's at the time, whose syndicate had insured part of the cargo that was damaged in the quake, is said to have cabled his San Francisco agent: "Pay all our policyholders in full irrespective of the terms of their policies."

The Committee of Lloyd's began to take steps to assure that its members' financial health was sound enough to meet claim payments. Individuals who wanted to become members were required to reveal their resources, to make deposits with the Corporation by way of security, and to submit audited accounts. Under the 1909 Assurance Companies Act, the first measure to regulate general insurance in the United Kingdom, the Lloyd's Society was required to make an annual report showing that all its members were financially solvent.

Foreigners were first admitted as members of Lloyd's in 1969 and women were admitted in the following year. Opening up the Society to women and foreigners was seen as a way of bringing in new capital in the wake of heavy losses caused by Hurricane Betsy in 1965. Other changes were also recommended by the commission set up to find ways to make Lloyd's more attractive to potential investors but these went unheeded. Then, after publication of the Fisher Report on self-regulation commissioned by Lloyd's itself, the Lloyd's Act of 1982 was passed. This provided for a council to govern the affairs of the Society and other reforms.

Lloyd's business, once limited to shipping, broadened to include all forms of transportation, including "motor" business. Non-marine (fire and general business insurance) was first accepted in the 1870s and aviation in 1911. Today, more than half of Lloyd's premium income comes from insuring or reinsuring transportation-related risks and about a quarter from property damage coverages. About a third of the world's aviation insurance is written at Lloyd's. Lloyd's is also a major player in the reinsurance market: More than one-third of its premium income comes from treaty reinsurance and between 10 percent and 15 percent from facultative reinsurance.

Although the United Kingdom is still the largest source of Lloyd's income, business now comes to Lloyd's from all over the world. The United States and Canada account for about one-third of premiums and mainland Europe for about one-sixth.

How the Lloyd's Marketplace Works

Lloyd's is a unique institution. It has an enormous influence on the international marketplace yet its 1993 premiums represented less than 3 percent of total premiums worldwide, a portion of the market smaller than that of many insurance companies. It is housed in one of the most modern-looking buildings in London and yet it still operates in much the same way it did 300 years ago. And in the public's mind, it is synonymous with insurance yet it is not an insurance company. It is a marketplace just like the coffeehouse that gave it its name.

Membership of Lloyd's: The underwriting members of Lloyd's, the insuring entities that pool their wealth to provide the capital to support insurance, are known as "Names." It is the individual Names that bear the underwriting risk, earning a profit or loss on their investment, not Lloyd's Society or Lloyd's Corporation.

(Although the terms are sometimes used interchangeably, the term Society of Lloyd's is usually used to denote Lloyd's underwriters collectively and the term Corporation is reserved for the administrative structure that provides the premises, staff and central services which enable Lloyd's marketplace to function effectively.)

Members fall into three categories. Those who are actively involved in the insurance business on a daily basis, either with Lloyd's itself or with insurance brokers or agencies, are called "working Names." Underwriting members who are not professionally associated with Lloyd's — who use Lloyd's solely as an investment vehicle — are called "external Names." More than 80 percent of members are external Names and external Names provide close to 90 percent of Lloyd's underwriting capacity. In 1994, membership of Lloyd's was opened for the first time to a third category: corporate Names.

While membership in Lloyd's is open to individuals of any nationality, members are predominately from the English-speaking world, mainly from the United Kingdom. In 1993, fewer than 10 percent of active members lived in the United States and Canada. Corporate members must be incorporated in the European Community, the United States, Australia, New Zealand, Japan or in one of the other jurisdictions that meet the Council's qualifying requirements.

Members of Lloyd's were traditionally people of considerable wealth. But beginning in the mid-1970s, small investors with just enough money to qualify for membership began to join Lloyd's. As the popularity of Lloyd's as an investment vehicle increased, the number of members grew rapidly, rising to a peak of more than 30,000 in 1988 from about 6,000 in the early 1970s, and around 4,000 in the 1950s. But high syndicate losses in the late 1980s drained the assets of many members, particularly smaller investors, and a substantial number were forced to withdraw from active underwriting. By 1993, the number of active Names had dropped to about 19,500.

New members, who must be elected to the Society, are introduced to Lloyd's by a members' agent. The members' agent guides them through the application process, advises them on the selection of syndicates and provides them with administrative services such as accounting. Members must provide documentation of their wealth as well as go through a formal interview process to ensure that they understand the nature of the liabilities they are about to assume.

Once elected into the Society, members select a membership category, based on their wealth. This dictates the maximum amount of risk they can underwrite for that year. In the parlance of Lloyd's, this is their overall premium limit — the maximum amount of premium income that can be accepted on their behalf. Not surprisingly, working Names tend to choose a lower membership category than external Names.

There is no limit to an individual's underwriting capacity. The previous limit of £3 million was dropped in 1993. While only a small percentage of members (in 1993, 5 percent of working and external members combined) select an underwriting capacity above £1 million, this group accounts for a substantial portion of the overall capacity.

To become a member of Lloyd's, individuals must show they have a minimum level of wealth. They are also required to establish "funds at Lloyd's" in proportion to the level of underwriting granted to them by the Council of Lloyd's. The amount of wealth and the ratio of funds at Lloyd's to premium income limits (generally 20-50 percent of the overall premium limit, depending on the liquidity of the assets and each individual's resources) are determined by the Council and are subject to review each year. In addition, members must maintain the required level of funds in approved assets. Failure to do so may result in a reduction of their overall premium income limit or their withdrawal from underwriting.

All premiums received on behalf of a member are deposited in Lloyd's Premiums Trust Fund and all claims and underwriting expenses, including reinsurance premiums and other costs of membership, are paid from it. Members continue to receive dividends and interest from the securities deposited at Lloyd's and they also receive their share of investment income from the Premiums Trust Fund but this is not included as part of the total in the syndicate's year-end financial results.

In addition, members contribute to Lloyd's Central Fund based on their premium income. The Central Fund is designed to meet the claim liabilities of insolvent members. It protects policyholders against the inability of individual members to pay their share of losses, a security mechanism necessary for Lloyd's to continue to attract business.

Each member participates in the market as a "sole trader," a British legal term similar to sole proprietor. Like sole proprietors, sole traders have unlimited liability for their business activities. To reduce their ultimate liability, an increasing number of members purchase personal stop loss reinsurance policies. These insurance contracts provide protection from losses above a deductible or retention up to a certain level but do not cap liability. Once the limit of the reinsurance policy has been reached, the member has to pay the remaining loss amounts out of his or her own assets, as shown in the example below.

Suppose a member, Paul Smith, has an overall premium level of £1 million. His stop loss policy has a 20 percent retention requirement and a stop loss limit of 50 percent. He would pay the first £200,000 (20 percent) of losses for the year. The reinsurer would pay the next £300,000 in losses (50 percent minus the 20 percent retention), and Smith would pay all losses above that level. See the diagram on the next page.

If the syndicates in which Smith participates experience a year of high losses — let's say there are two hurricanes in the United States, several oil rigs sink in the Atlantic and there is a spate of airplane crashes — claims may greatly exceed Smith's £1 million premium limit.

Stop Loss Policy

	Smith	Unlimited liability
50% of £1 million	Reinsurer	£300,000
	Smith	£200,000 (20% of £1 million)

Members' obligation to pay claims on business underwritten on their behalf continues "down to their last cuff links," they are warned when they join the Society, or after women were admitted, "down to their last pair of earrings." It only ceases when all their assets, with the exception of a modest home, have been turned over to Lloyd's.

Members participate in the insurance marketplace through syndicates, a mechanism through which they can pool their money. Syndicates generally are known by the name of their managing agent or lead underwriter and are assigned a number that is used on all insurance policies and other official documents.

Members participate in the underwriting of every risk accepted on behalf of the syndicate. Likewise, they also share in the syndicate's profits and losses. These are calculated based on the amount of money each member contributed to the syndicate's total capacity. To spread the risk of loss, each member now participates in many different syndicates. In 1993, the average member joined in 19 syndicates, up from 10 in 1983. The average participation or "line" per syndicate was £23,787. In the 1980s, there were more than 400 different syndicates. But, by 1994, a series of consolidations had reduced the number to 179, at the same time increasing the average premium capacity or syndicate "stamp." The amount of premium income is monitored to prevent syndicates from taking on more risk than their members have chosen to underwrite.

Members delegate the management and underwriting of their insurance business to managing agents who run the syndicates. The managing agent employs the "active" underwriter, the insurance professional who accepts risks on behalf of the members, and other staff, and keeps the syndicate's accounts and records. To promote prudent underwriting, active underwriters are required to participate as members in their own syndicates.

A syndicate is not a legal entity but simply "an annual venture" in which a group of individual members come together to do business for administrative convenience. Members must notify their managing agent by a certain date if they plan to terminate their agreement with the agent at the end of the year and managing agents must notify a member if they no longer wish to act as an agent for that individual in the syndicates they manage. Once agreements with managing agents are dissolved, members are free to shift their capital to other syndicates for the following calendar year. If the syndicate has no plans to reduce its underwriting, the retiring member's capacity is taken up by an incoming member. But the outgoing member remains liable for claims on insurance policies written on his or her behalf in previous years.

The Accounting Period and Its Effect on Members: Lloyd's currently operates on a three-year accounting period. (There has been some discussion of reducing this in some cases to two.) Although syndicates have a one-year constitution, the financial results of their operations are not calculated until after an additional two years. This means that a new member will not receive his or her share of underwriting and investment profit from the Premiums Trust Fund for at least three and a half years after becoming a member.

This unique accounting system is thought to date back to medieval times. Voyages took much longer then even if the crossing was uneventful. But many ships went off course or were delayed by bad weather. Presumably, any ship that had not returned by the end of three years was given up for lost, allowing merchants to total up their profits and losses.

Because Lloyd's syndicates are not on-going businesses like other insurance entities, they cannot hold reserves for future claims beyond the end of the accounting period. But some claims may not have been settled or even reported at this point. To ensure funds are available to pay these claims, a reinsurance contract, "reinsurance to close," is drawn up at the end of the three-year period by the successor syndicate for the underwriting year or "year of account." This reinsures members' liability for losses in the underwriting year that is being closed and protects members of the successor syndicate against those liabilities.

However, it is not always possible to arrive at an accurate determination of future liabilities even after three years. This is especially true when the risks insured were primarily long-tail liability. These are loss exposures with latent liabilities like environmental pollution and asbestos-related diseases where the harm may not be apparent (and thus claims may not be filed) until a decade or more after the insurance policy was issued. When it is impossible to make an estimate of the profitability of any underwriting year, and hence the amount of reinsurance needed, the period until the account is closed is called "open years" or the "run-off years of account." Management of open years of account is the responsibility of the managing agent, who may hire a specialist agency to close the account.

Since members may only leave a syndicate when their liabilities have been covered with a reinsurance contract, members involved in open years cannot resign from a syndicate or the Society of Lloyd's until these accounts are closed.

In 1993, there were about 11,000 inactive members. Managing agents closing account years may continue to call on members for additional cash if there is a deficiency.

The Insurance Transaction

The general public and commercial entities seeking insurance at Lloyd's have no direct access to Lloyd's underwriters although insurance buyers nowadays sometimes accompany their brokers. With the exception of some U.K. automobile insurance, only a broker accredited by the Council can place business in Lloyd's market on behalf of clients. Most of the world's largest insurance brokerage firms own a

Lloyd's subsidiary. At the beginning of 1994, some 230 firms of brokers were permitted access to Lloyd's market, a figure that includes not only the brokerage firms owned by large corporations such as Marsh & McLennan but also the small specialist brokers with only a handful of employees that specialize by territory or product.

In the past, some underwriting syndicates were owned or controlled by Lloyd's brokers acting as managing agents. This created the potential for a serious conflict of interest. There are stories of a few unscrupulous brokers setting up syndicates on which they placed their friends. They brought their most lucrative business to these syndicates, regardless of whether they could get better terms for their clients elsewhere and took the riskiest business to syndicates made up primarily of external members. There were also brokers who pressured their syndicates' underwriters into taking business that the underwriter would otherwise have refused. To prevent such abuses, legislation was enacted in 1982 that required brokers to divest themselves of the ownership or control of managing agencies by 1987.

Lloyd's brokers today function in much the same way as they did in the early days of the coffeehouse. The broker is responsible for preparing the documentation or slip used to present key underwriting information to underwriters in the Underwriting Room, or The Room as it is often called, and for securing their initials and line — the portion of the risk they accept. The Lloyd's slip, a stiff document rather like cardboard, is essentially the contract of insurance. Besides the details of the risk to be insured and the name of the client, the slip includes the amount of insurance and any coverage restrictions.

Active underwriters for each syndicate and their staff are stationed around the huge room at desks known as "boxes." Brokers, carrying the slip, line up to speak to the underwriters most likely to be interested in underwriting the risk that they are presenting on behalf of their clients. They may also call on underwriters to negotiate terms on business already discussed or to close on it.

A typical risk will be placed with a number of syndicates, but the broker must first seek out a lead underwriter, a person who is recognized by the market as having special expertise in the kinds of loss exposures to be insured. The lead underwriter usually sets the premium rate and conditions, approves the policy language and often, but not always, underwrites the largest line.

Once a lead underwriter has been found and has initialed, or "scratched" the slip on behalf of the syndicate, the slip is presented to "following" underwriters, those who agree to follow the terms specified by the lead underwriter, until the loss exposure is fully subscribed. As soon as the syndicate's number has been stamped next to the underwriter's signature, the syndicate is contractually bound. Usually, underwriters reinsure portions of the loss exposures they have accepted, often with other Lloyd's syndicates.

Lloyd's brokers, or London brokers as they are sometimes called, are not restricted to the Lloyd's marketplace. When the risk is large or exceptionally difficult to insure, a broker may not be able to get all the insurance needed from Lloyd's syndicates. In such cases, brokers may seek out insurers in other segments of the insurance market to assume part of the risk.

The London insurance market is made up of Lloyd's and hundreds of insurers that comprise the Company market. Like Lloyd's, the London Company market tends to be separated into marine and non-marine business. Many foreign insurers also participate in the London market, usually through underwriting agencies, which are authorized to underwrite specific types and specified amounts of insurance on behalf of the insurance companies they represent.

When all the necessary commitments to insure the risk have been obtained, the broker issues a "cover note" informing the client that the risk is insured. The note also sets out the basic terms and conditions of the insurance policy and the percentage of the risk accepted by each syndicate.

Later, often some time after the cover note has been sent, the broker prepares the insurance policy which is forwarded, along with the slip, to the Lloyd's Policy Signing Office (LPSO). LPSO checks the written details of the transaction and signs the policy on behalf of all the syndicates involved before sending it to the client but the broker remains responsible for any errors. (Underwriters rarely see the policies they have underwritten unless there is a claim.) Besides verifying and processing insurance policies, LPSO maintains the central accounting system, which debits and credits brokers' and underwriters' accounts as policies are issued.

Once the insurance policy is in force, the broker becomes legally liable for payment of the premium within the time frame laid out by the underwriter. The broker is also responsible for presenting claims to the syndicates and managing the claim settlement process.

The New Business Plan

Lloyd's syndicates were hit by enormous losses between 1988 and 1991, due in part to a huge number of asbestos and pollution-related claims and damage caused by violent windstorms in Europe and the United States. The total underwriting loss for those four years was a staggering £7.4 billion. By comparison, underwriting profits for the previous 17 years, 1970-1987, amounted to £4.91 billion.

These massive losses forced an unprecedented number of Names into or near personal bankruptcy and prompted many others to reconsider their association with Lloyd's, seriously depleting the market's insurance capacity. In addition, in a much publicized battle with the institution, groups of Lloyd's members, involving thousands of Names, decided to take legal action to recoup or at least preserve their assets. Names' unhappiness was compounded by their inability to resign as long as the syndicates in which they participated still had open years.

The magnitude of the losses and their impact on Lloyd's members and the insurance community prompted calls for immediate action to correct the deficiencies that appeared to have contributed to the crisis. In 1991, a task force was formed under the chairmanship of David Rowland to consider solutions to Lloyd's diminishing underwriting capacity. (Mr. Rowland is now chairman of Lloyd's.) In January 1992, it published its report, "Lloyd's: A Route Forward." Like other commissions formed to devise ways to attract new members, it didn't limit its recommendations to strengthening Lloyd's capital base. Among other things, it suggested a new structure for governing and changes in how the institution functioned aimed at improving Lloyd's competitiveness in the world marketplace.

As mentioned earlier, the 1982 Lloyd's Act provided for a council to govern the affairs of the Society. However, this form of governance, which allowed the council to both regulate the conduct of the market and at the same time advance the Society's business interests, came in for severe criticism.

Among the first of the task force's recommendations to be implemented was the separation of regulatory and business responsibilities. Lloyd's now has three governing bodies: the Council of Lloyd's, which remains the sovereign body; the Regulatory Board, which is responsible for the effective regulation of the market; and the Market Board, which deals with business issues.

To expand its capital base and at the same time build confidence in the future of Lloyd's, the task force recommended that Lloyd's open its doors to corporate Names. Corporate members were admitted beginning with the 1994 account year. The requirements for corporations, which, unlike individual Names, have limited liability for losses, are somewhat different than for individuals. Corporate members are required to deposit assets equal to 50 percent of their overall premium limit rather than the typical 30 percent for individuals and are assessed at a rate that is two and a half times that of individual members for contributions to the Central Fund —the fund that pays the outstanding claims of insolvent members.

In 1994, corporate capital came from 12 investment trusts trading on the London Stock Exchange, which raised about £800 million, and 13 individual companies, which invested a total of £100 million. Together, they added £1.6 billion in capacity to Lloyd's syndicates, 15 percent of the £10.9 billion total.

Besides introducing corporate entities, Lloyd's created new kinds of membership to attract more individual Names and to provide a better match between members' participation and their wealth and income.

One new membership category is the Members' Agents Pooling Arrangement (MAPA). MAPA, which is something akin to a mutual fund, is intended to reduce the volatility of results, ensuring a steady flow of income to members rather than roller coaster years of alternating high profits and losses. MAPAs allow members' agents to pool all or a part of their Names' underwriting capacity and thus participate in a wider spread of syndicates than is possible with individual portfolios. One feature of MAPAs is that Names participating in this arrangement can have a higher overall premium limit relative to funds deposited than in standard syndicate participation because the smaller lines and greater level of diversification lower the risk of high losses. In 1994, MAPAs represented more than half of Lloyd's capital base.

Other membership changes are designed to appeal to the wealthiest individuals.

Lloyd's has also taken steps to deal with the "open" or "old years," as they are now called. By the end of 1995, Lloyd's expects to have reinsured all individual members' liabilities for policies written prior to 1986, thus allowing Names who wish to do so to retire and protecting current and future members from liabilities dating back to that time. To accomplish this task, Lloyd's will create a new reinsurance company, dubbed Newco initially and now called Equitas, to assume the reserves and liabilities associated with risks insured before 1986 that are still held on syndicates' books.

Other reforms promote higher professional standards among those who work at Lloyd's, cut costs and seek to change management styles.

Under consideration is some kind of market mechanism to regulate the supply and demand for capital, ensure the efficient allocation of capital within the market, and help open up access to the most successful syndicates. One option is to place a value on syndicate participation, by requiring members to pay a certain amount to join each syndicate rather than just signing up as is now the case. The greater the demand to join a particular syndicate, the higher the price would be. Another possible alternative is for members to buy capacity from other members seeking to leave the syndicate and to assume the potential for profit or loss on the open years. In addition, individual Names may soon have the opportunity to participate in underwriting at Lloyd's on a limited liability basis through a scheme which would create individual corporate members.

Some observers believe that Lloyd's recent troubles stemmed in large part from its failure to adapt to the current business environment. Thus, traditional ways of doing business are still being evaluated and the process of rebuilding will continue beyond these initial innovations. But while Lloyd's is being restructured for the future, the strengths it inherited from the past will be retained and even enhanced. In making recommendations for change to restore confidence in Lloyd's, the Rowland Task Force took pains to maintain its historical framework. As Mr. Rowland wrote in the task force report, "Because Lloyd's is such an extraordinarily complex market with major advantages derived from its history, great care is needed to ensure that the pressure for necessary change is not allowed to damage the very fabric it is seeking to preserve."

Will changes now being implemented restore Lloyd's to its former eminence? A report issued in December 1994 by Chatset Ltd., a London firm of financial analysts, suggests that Lloyd's syndicates are seriously underreserved. The full extent of Names' outstanding liabilities, mainly for future claims involving asbestos and pollution, will become clearer when Equitas has completed its task of evaluating reserves in preparation for reinsuring pre-1986 liabilities. It will then be possible to judge how grave a threat to the Society's future these losses are.

6 Changes in the Reinsurance Environment

By Gerald F. Fisher
Vice President and Special Counsel
North American Reinsurance Corporation

One of the few certainties in the reinsurance environment over the past decade has been the certainty of change. New challenges have arisen almost continuously in an environment unprecedented in its demands on reinsurers. Potential losses, especially from catastrophes, have soared. The price tag for environmental liability continues to grow and competition in the reinsurance market shows no sign of moderating. In addition, external factors, such as taxation and regulation, are exerting ever greater influence on company decision-making and operations.

These changes and many others have transformed the reinsurance industry. They require fundamental shifts in capital deployment and management philosophy. Even the relationships with ceding companies, the reinsurer's clients, are being altered substantially.

This chapter will discuss some of the factors that brought about these changes and explore the impact that they have had upon reinsurers.

Increased Risk Exposure

In many respects, the reinsurance industry and the primary insurance industry face similar problems. Both, for example, have experienced growth in potential losses or risk exposures, a long-term trend that shows no sign of abating. The increase, which arises from tort liability as well as property insurance coverages, can be seen in the volume of civil litigation, the size of average jury awards, the number and dollar amount of insurance company claim payments and, in recent years, high catastrophe losses. This last factor, the rising cost of natural disasters, has brought the increase in risk exposures to everyone's notice.

Adverse developments in the U.S. legal environment have contributed significantly to this expansion of liability. For example, in product liability cases a negligence standard of liability has gradually been replaced with a standard of strict liability. To receive damages, all the plaintiff need prove is that the product defect caused the injury. The presence or absence of negligence on the part of the plaintiff is irrelevant. In many states, the contributory negligence rule, which bars compensation if there was any negligence on the part of the plaintiff, has given way to the concept of comparative negligence. Under this legal doctrine plaintiffs may recover according to their degree of fault in the accident. For example, if a plaintiff was found to have been the cause of 40 percent of his injury, he could still collect 60 percent from the defendant.

Another factor that has pushed up claim payments in tort cases has been the application of the rule of joint and several liability. Under this rule, any defendant found to have contributed in any way to an injury may be held liable for the entire amount of damages. In cases where there is only one solvent defendant, the usual remedy of court-ordered contribution from others who contributed to the injury is useless. This change has caused plaintiffs' attorneys to sue all conceivable parties, even parties unknown at the time the suit is filed, to preserve all possible future claims and avoid subsequent charges of malpractice. Consequently the scale, expense and procedural complexity of virtually all tort litigation have risen geometrically.

Some legal developments have evolved out of the need to assess liability for injuries arising from emerging technologies and the goods produced through use of these technologies. Advances in transportation and communication have promoted the globalization of industries. Globalization creates a worldwide market for new products, many of which pose dangers to their users that are currently unknown or are not effectively communicated. In addition, many manufacturing processes and raw materials extraction and processing operations generate wastes that are proving to be hazardous to life on this planet.

Unfortunately, these dangers sometimes are not fully understood until many years or decades after the products have been put to general use. And even more distressing, some manufacturers, motivated by the desire for continued profits, have persisted in making certain products despite data internally communicated to management suggesting possible health risks. The history of asbestos is the most notorious example of this disregard for safety, but it is by no means unique.

Asbestos was widely used as a building material and in many industrial applications, such as automobile brake linings. Although we now recognize, with hindsight, that there were signs that asbestos could cause disease, the problem was not widely acknowledged until the 1960s. The story of hazardous wastes has been similar and the current investigation of tobacco product manufacturing may turn up the same problem.

The injuries caused by asbestos and other toxic substances — so-called toxic torts — have given rise to complex and often costly lawsuits. These, in turn, have prompted companies being sued to attempt to reconstruct their insurance policies over a period of many years to determine whether they have insurance coverage for the injuries and property damage for which they might be liable. Injuries and property damage caused by environmental pollution are most commonly addressed by liability insurance. This exposure also may be covered by the debris removal provisions of property insurance policies. Fires and explosions release toxic substances into the environment and the cost of neutralizing or removing these wastes, often recovered under property insurance policies, has been a subject of major concern.

Beyond the highly publicized dangers to public health and safety arising from the use of new materials and new technologies, such mundane developments as the expansion of municipal liability have affected the primary insurance industry and, consequently, the reinsurance industry as well. Coverage for municipal liability has been difficult to obtain because of a combination of several factors, including the erosion of traditional doctrines of governmental immunity from tort liability and the expansion of municipal services into areas where the doctrine of governmental immunity does not apply, such as recreational facilities and other activities which are similar to private sector activities.

The expansion and changes in the types of liability which insurers have been called upon to address have been accompanied by an increase in the amount of time between the period for which an insurance policy is issued and the period in which claims are reported. This is commonly referred to as the long tail of liability. Since insurance and reinsurance must be priced long before the cost is known, this time gap makes the pricing of liability insurance and reinsurance extremely difficult.

The growth in risk exposure has also accelerated because of the increase in the value of property to be insured. This trend is evident to anyone in the market for a house or a new car. But the escalation in values exposed to risk of loss is not confined to personal items. Businesses are experiencing a similar phenomenon. An extreme example is the Piper Alpha oil drilling platform, which was destroyed in a storm in the North Sea in 1988 and cost insurers and reinsurers $1.2 billion.

With the rise in values has also come a greater geographic concentration of values. The population of the United States has been drifting toward the south and the east and west coasts for many years. As a result, there has been extensive development of coastal areas for both residential and commercial purposes. This growth has taken place despite the vulnerability of these areas to natural disasters in the form of hurricanes on the Atlantic and Gulf coasts and earthquakes in regions near the Pacific coast. Seismologists warn that a major earthquake is likely to shake the West coast within the next two decades and the New Madrid fault in southern Missouri may shake the center of the continent again, as it did in 1811.

Beyond the expansion of tort liability and the increase in amounts and concentrations of values to be insured, both insurers and reinsurers have had to face a legal system that appears to see insurance companies as a "deep pocket" — a way of funding any and all claims for damages brought before the courts. Whether or not this perception is accurate depends on one's analysis and interpretation of the mass of conflicting information on the subject. Each observer tends to see the data through the filter of his or her own prejudices and preconceptions. But it is clear that the funding role of the insurance industry is significant.

A more fundamental problem for the insurance industry lies in the legal system's lack of predictability. American legal scholars and professionals view the ability of the courts to fashion new remedies and indeed to create new laws as one of the glories of our common law system. Consider, for example, the 1916 landmark case of MacPherson vs. Buick Motor Co. When a lower court held that the owner of an automobile could not sue the manufacturer of that automobile for a defect which caused an accident, because there was no privity of contract (legal relationship) between the owner and the manufacturer, the Court of Appeals of the State of New York simply abolished the defense of privity of contract for manufactured products. As long as the courts have the power to create and abolish rules of law, whether they relate to privity of contract or contributory negligence or, more recently, the right to an abortion, the legal system will not have the degree of predictability which insurers and reinsurers once assumed it had. In retrospect, we can see that the legal system never had the degree of predictability that many believed it possessed, but it is only in recent years that insurers and reinsurers have begun to understand this fact of legal life.

Impact on Reinsurers of Increased Risk Exposure

The growth in loss exposures faced by primary insurers has a profound impact on reinsurers. Much of the increased risk in underwriting these exposures is being transferred to reinsurers as the result of basic changes in the reinsurance business itself. One such trend has been the enormous growth in facultative reinsurance.

Facultative reinsurance developed out of a practice common 25 years ago of making special "acceptances" — agreeing to cover risks not covered by treaty reinsurance terms — and since then, it has grown to be a major segment of the reinsurance business. As is explained elsewhere in this book, facultative reinsurance is priced by the reinsurer on a risk-by-risk basis. The reinsurer's pricing is independent of the ceding company's pricing and there is no mechanism for sharing the results of a line of business as there is in treaty reinsurance.

Another long-term trend is the shift in treaty reinsurance from pro rata to excess forms of reinsurance. Largely the result of a desire to reduce the constant flow of money between the ceding and assuming companies, excess-of-loss reinsurance gives the reinsurer fewer dollars for a risk exposure that is potentially much greater.

Over the years the growth of facultative and excess-of-loss forms of reinsurance, at the expense of treaty and pro rata, has undermined the "partnership" nature of reinsurance so typical of reinsurance relationships in the past. Recently, ceding company retentions have increased as large fluctuations in the price and amount of reinsurance available caused changes in management philosophy. This, too, has increased the underwriting risk to which reinsurers are exposed by reducing the portion of reinsurance in working layers (levels of coverage at which frequent but predictable small losses occur). This leaves reinsurers with fewer dollars for larger amounts of potential risk exposure in the higher layers. In the uppermost layers, reinsurance premiums may be only a few dollars per thousand dollars of coverage. A group of claims arising from a common cause, such as asbestos, or from a single occurrence, such as Hurricane Andrew, can consume many years' worth of premiums.

Responses to Increased Risk Exposure

Reinsurers have encouraged primary insurers to address those aspects of increased risk which are passed along to reinsurers, but the results so far have been limited. At the state level, the passage of tort reform measures has been uneven and at the federal level, efforts to reform product liability law, have been unsuccessful so far. However, that may change in the Republican-controlled 104th Congress.

Primary insurers' attempts to limit their liability through changes in contractual terms also have had mixed results. The claims-made policy, which some believed would facilitate the underwriting of long tail lines of business, has not been widely accepted either in the marketplace or by regulators and the courts. Reactions to other measures designed to reduce risk exposures, such as the adoption of additional coverage exclusions, have been similar. The best known of these, the gradual pollution exclusion incorporated into commercial liability policies, has been dealt with harshly by both legislators and the courts.

The reinsurance industry has taken much the same approach to these problems. The result is reflected in reinsurance contract terms and in reinsurance program structures. Reinsurers have sought to limit their liabilities to ceding companies with long lists of exclusions. These efforts, like those of the primary insurers, have met with limited acceptance. Likewise, the reinsurance equivalent of the claims-made policy, a "sunset" clause, under which all claims must be presented by the ceding company to the reinsurer within a limited period of time, typically four or five years, encountered considerable resistance in the marketplace. The sunset clause is part of what is sometimes referred to as "non-traditional" or "finite risk" reinsurance, which includes various other limitations to protect the reinsurer.

In the last decade a common response to these problems has been withdrawal from the business. In some cases the withdrawal has been involuntary as reinsurers, both domestic and foreign, have become insolvent. The most spectacular insolvency has been that of Mission Insurance, which was heavily involved in the reinsurance business and was reported to be insolvent by hundreds of millions of dollars. It is important to remember that most reinsurers have not become insolvent and indeed many of them, as a result of the turnaround in rates in the mid 1980s, are in good financial condition.

Both before and after the cycle turned, many reinsurers withdrew from specific segments of the market. They cut back operations to levels which their management believed they could effectively control, or they simply withdrew from those segments of the reinsurance business that appeared to offer an inadequate return for the capital and management time invested in them. One notable example of withdrawal from the market was the sale by one reinsurance company of its life reinsurance affiliate so that it could concentrate on its highly successful property and casualty reinsurance business. Another has been the withdrawal by many Names at Lloyd's. Due to high losses and other problems, some syndicates either merged or exited from the marketplace. The events at Lloyd's have also led to attempts to develop new systems and structures for managing the runoff of long tail liability losses.

Primary insurers also have withdrawn from segments of the primary market, raising concerns about availability. These concerns have been communicated to lawmakers in testimony before legislative committees and in regulatory hearings. In the past, availability problems typically were addressed by the creation of residual market mechanisms, such as automobile assigned risk plans and coastal windstorm pools, but in the case of marketplace disruptions following the very large losses from Hurricane Andrew, a different response was required. The residual market merely shares the risk among primary insurers. What was needed after Hurricane Andrew was a mechanism to fund the risk since reinsurers, the traditional risk spreaders, were also pulling back from the property insurance marketplace. Thus, in 1993, the Florida Hurricane Catastrophe Fund — in effect, a state-sponsored reinsurer — was established.

Some developments in the marketplace, the withdrawal from municipal liability insurance by primary insurers, for example, have been approached differently. The preferred solution has been to set up organizations of various kinds that specialize in insuring particular types of risks. These organizations —captives, risk retention groups or other risk-sharing mechanisms — are in reality specialty insurers that compete with primary insurers and are taking a substantial volume of business away from them. They often turn to reinsurers in the traditional marketplace for reinsurance coverage. Since those specialty insurers are relatively small, they are likely to buy more reinsurance than a larger primary company writing the same underlying risks. Thus, if a reinsurer has the skills to underwrite the type of business involved, the displacement of risk exposure from the primary insurers to the specialty insurers represents a business opportunity for the reinsurer.

Less Room for Error

The reinsurance industry was placed in the public spotlight as a result of an antitrust action by the attorneys general of 20 states. In 1988, the attorneys general charged that insurers and domestic and foreign reinsurers had conspired to create a global boycott of certain liability coverages, particularly coverage for environmental damages stemming from pollution. The U.S. Supreme Court reviewed the case and in June 1993 it said the plaintiffs would have to prove their allegations under the court's narrow definition of the term "boycott." The case has recently been settled, but this action exemplifies another characteristic of the new environment in which the reinsurance business must operate. This is what might be called "the reduced margin for error." Regardless of the substance of the antitrust charges, it is clear that the reinsurance business is now subject to a far greater degree of scrutiny than it was in the past. As our business, which was once almost unknown outside the insurance industry, receives increasing attention, significant errors of judgment are unlikely to be ignored by the courts.

While risk exposures have increased for insurers, in general, and for reinsurers, in particular, the resources to meet these increased risk exposures have diminished. The capital structure of major commercial lines insurers usually includes substantial amounts of "reinsurance recoverable" — payments anticipated from reinsurers on claims covered by reinsurance contracts — and the capital structure of many reinsurers includes large amounts of "retrocession recoverable" — the reinsurance of reinsurance contracts. Accurate information covering the whole insurance industry is not readily available but the amounts are substantial.

To the extent that this reinsurance is not recoverable, the industry's policyholder surplus is reduced. Similarly, the reinsurance industry has much of its surplus offset by retrocessions recoverable from other reinsurers. This fragility of capital is illustrated by the number of reinsurers, both large and small, that have collapsed or shut down their operations in the last decade. In addition, the closing of the insurance exchanges in New York and Florida demonstrate that alternative structures, specially established to conduct reinsurance business, are exposed to the same kinds of problems as reinsurers organized in the usual corporate fashion. The ultimate retrocession recoverable problem arose from the LMX spiral in Lloyd's and other participants in the London market where the same business was reinsured several times by the same players who later became insolvent. The extent of this kind of abuse is not at all clear but that it happened at all makes it difficult to determine the financial condition of hundreds of Lloyd's syndicates and the many thousand Names (individual investors) who participated in them.

Competition

Although capital weakness has reduced flexibility and the margin for error, competition among reinsurers remains strong. There has been a surge of new entrants to the reinsurance marketplace in the last few years. Much of this increase is to be found offshore. A recent Reinsurance Association of America study found that in 1991 U.S. insurers ceded $8.2 billion in premiums to overseas reinsurers, a rise of 35 percent over the amount ceded to non-U.S. companies in the prior year.

Bermuda companies accounted for nearly a third of the overseas market, receiving $2.5 billion in premiums from U.S. insurers. The United Kingdom was a close second with $2.4 billion and Barbados was third with $802 million in premiums.

These newly-established companies appear to be different from the companies that came into the marketplace in the 1960s and 1970s. The current offshore entities are far more narrowly focused and appear to have much higher levels of expertise. The new entrants of the 1960s and 1970s usually had modest capitalization (many under $50 million) and accepted most of their business from brokers with, we now see, little underwriting effort. The more recent arrivals have large capitalization (typically several hundred million dollars) and appear to be hiring people with high levels of technical expertise for underwriting business in a self-imposed limited range.

In addition to financial capital, human capital — reinsurance expertise — is also readily available. In the 1960s and the 1970s, new reinsurers were typically established by people recruited from the handful of existing reinsurers. By contrast, today there is a large pool of experienced individuals with specialized knowledge of various types of reinsurance which makes entry into the reinsurance business relatively easy. This ease of entry remains one of the most remarkable facets of the business.

Reinsurance brokers are major players in the property and casualty reinsurance business. They help ensure a high degree of competition. Traditionally, roughly three-quarters of the property and casualty reinsurance business as measured by premium volume, has been handled by brokers, leaving about one quarter to the direct-writing professional reinsurers. Brokers' share of the business dropped somewhat in the market turnaround in the mid-1980s, but this does not appear to have substantially diminished their role in the reinsurance marketplace. The resulting competition has pushed rates down more rapidly than many had expected. Whether this decline puts rates at a level commensurate with the risks being assumed, considering the efforts by both reinsurers and primary insurers to limit their exposure as discussed above, remains to be seen.

Financial Markets

The reinsurance industry is not isolated from other sectors of the financial industry. Indeed, in recent years the lines that once separated various segments have become increasingly blurred. Thus, stresses in other sectors, such as the precipitous decline in stock market values in October 1987 and the decline in interest rates in 1992 have had an impact on the reinsurance business and also have reduced the room for error. Fortunately, the fluctuations in the stock market appear to have had little direct impact on most reinsurers.

For the insurance and reinsurance business, however, a far more serious problem has been the volatility of interest rates over the past decade. The extremely high interest rates of the late 1970s and early 1980s was one of the factors that led insurers and reinsurers into "cash flow" underwriting, which put greater emphasis on generating cash flow for investment purposes at the expense of traditional underwriting strategies. When interest rates declined, those who had espoused earnings on reserves were left exposed to cash shortfalls because earnings on reserves were substantially lower than had been expected at the time the policies were written. This reinvestment risk can have a severe impact on investment earnings from long tail reserves. And because reinsurer's reserves typically have longer tails than primary insurer reserves, interest rate volatility has a greater effect on the financial results of reinsurers than primary insurers.

This decline in investment income has been somewhat masked by realization of capital gains from the sale of higher yielding bonds. This is, however, a short term and non-recurring benefit. Those who have sold securities are left with lower yielding investments which will either hold down profits or reduce mitigation of losses until after interest rates rise substantially and new cash flows can be invested instead of being used to pay claims currently due.

The problems faced by the banking industry, another segment of the mammoth financial services industry, also have had an impact on reinsurers. Banks and savings and loan associations in the United States have been through the most financially devastating period since the early 1930s. The practical effect of the banking industry's troubles on the reinsurance business has been the imposition of capital adequacy requirements for letters of credit issued by banks. This has increased the price charged for these letters. The importance of letters of credit, which are widely used to support "alien" (non-U.S.) reinsurance, is discussed in greater detail later in this book.

The financial pressures and strains affecting other sectors have contributed to efforts by all participants in the financial services industry to broaden the scope of their activities in the hope of expanding their earnings base or decreasing their business risks through diversification. The result is new competition in each financial services sector. This gradual erosion of the barriers separating the various specialties which make up the financial services industry has generated new competition and, through a domino effect, poses potential new threats to the solvency of the whole system.

Another potential danger, inflation, has been relatively subdued in recent years. In the 1970s and early 1980s, inflation — both economic and social — had a severe impact on the reinsurance industry as it drove ever-increasing numbers of claims into higher layers of reinsurance. Reinsurers tried to meet the threat of inflation by indexing retentions in reinsurance treaties so that they would move up with the rise in prices, but these measures were not well accepted in the marketplace. While at the time of this writing inflation appears to have abated, some observers see signs of rising inflation ahead.

The most recent development having an impact across traditional business lines is the rise of derivatives. At this time the direct impact of derivatives on the reinsurance business has been minimal. While it does not appear to be displacing traditional reinsurance, in the years ahead, one form of derivative, the insurance futures contract, could compete directly with reinsurance. The greatest impact of derivatives on insurers generally has been the realization of the danger some derivatives, such as collateralized mortgage obligations, may pose for the investment portfolios of life insurers. This has caused the National Association of Insurance Commissioners to consider substantive changes to both the regulation of such investments and enhancements to the rules for their disclosure and valuation in financial statements.

Taxation

Increased federal taxation as a result of changes brought about by the Tax Reform Act of 1986 is another factor constricting the margin for error of the reinsurance industry. For many years, federal income taxation of property and casualty insurance and reinsurance was very closely tied to statutory accounting. The conservative nature of statutory accounting resulted in what was perceived, by some critics, to be a substantial tax benefit for the insurance and reinsurance business.

As a result of the 1986 income tax law changes, property and casualty reinsurers now must discount loss reserves for tax purposes. Consequently, they must anticipate the investment income that they will earn on investments held for their reserves. Also, 20 percent of any increase in unearned premium reserves is subject to taxation. The scope of these changes is beyond this discussion, but it is important to understand that it has had effects on the way insurers and reinsurers conduct their business. The tax on increases in reserves for unearned premiums has caused insurers to issue short term (for example, semi-annual) policies. The discounting provision is forcing almost all insurers to show taxable income in their tax returns, thereby forcing them to raise prices or accept a lower after-tax return on equity. Since reinsurers are usually more heavily reserved than primary insurers because of the long tail nature of their liabilities, discounting reserves for tax purposes represents a significant cost to reinsurers (a 7 percent charge on premiums by one estimate). This has encouraged the reinsurance of business generating long tail reserves with companies in jurisdictions outside the United States, where tax treatment is more favorable or where there is, at least, some congruity between taxation accounting and accounting for financial statement presentation.

Rising Expectations

Traditionally, reinsurance has not been an industry that attracted much public or even regulatory and legislative interest. In recent years, however, the demands of virtually everyone who deals with the reinsurance industry have created what might be termed a climate of "rising expectations."

These increased demands upon reinsurance have emanated from regulators, professionals whose work is impacted by reinsurance, legislators, attorneys general, ceding companies and ultimately the general public.

Regulatory concerns about reinsurance have escalated enormously over the course of the last decade because of the growing number and size of insolvencies. In the 1970s and even earlier, the National Association of Insurance Commissioners (NAIC) dealt with the subject of reinsurance on a sporadic basis. Since that time reinsurance has come to permeate many aspects of the commissioners' work. The NAIC's first concern is for the solvency of primary insurers. Reinsurance recoverables represent such an important component of the assets of primary insurers that commissioners must pay careful attention to the value and collectibility of reinsurance as an asset.

This concern with issues relating to solvency, including accounting, reserving, investments and reinsurance, represents a fundamental shift from the commissioners' traditional concern with issues relating to rates, forms and sales and claims practices. Surprisingly, however, this has not led them to be more sympathetic to measures, such as the acceptance of the claims-made policy form, that attempt to address fundamental underwriting problems. Instead, the commissioners have sought more data on reinsurance and have issued substantive regulations affecting reinsurance transactions.

Specifically, new schedules have been added to the annual financial statement to provide more information on loss development, including the loss development of assumed reinsurance. Also, the reinsurance recoverable schedules of the annual statement have been modified to show the extent of what potentially is uncollectible by requiring the "aging" of receivables. In addition to seeking more information, the commissioners are also seeking to have this information provided to them in ways that enable them to use it more quickly and easily. These include requiring annual statements to be filed in a computer-readable form so that each statement can be rapidly analyzed for signs of potential financial difficulty.

Over time the commissioners have issued various regulations which impact substantively on reinsurance. The first such action was taken many years ago to reverse the result of the Pink case [Fidelity & Deposit Company vs. Pink, 32 U.S. 224 (1937)] and to require use of what is now considered the standard insolvency clause. This clause enables the receiver of an insolvent insurer to collect reinsurance.

Several years ago, the insolvencies of Mission, Transit Insurance Company and others led Congressman John Dingell of Michigan to instigate an investigation of the insurance business. The result was a report, *Failed Promises*, which was strongly critical of state regulation. Dingell went on to propose several new laws for federal regulation of insurance. As of this writing, these proposals have won little support in Congress but have prompted action by the commissioners.

The NAIC has used *Failed Promises* as a starting point for reforming state regulation. Problems with uncollectible reinsurance were an important theme in *Failed Promises*. This and other criticisms caused the NAIC to develop new and improved model laws governing credit for reinsurance (of greatest concern for ceding insurers buying reinsurance from reinsurers not licensed in the United States), fronting (the ceding of much of the risk and some element of control to the reinsurer), intermediaries (both brokers and managing general agents) and assumption reinsurance (a life insurance issue).

The NAIC has also improved state regulation by exercising its quasi-legislative powers through the Annual Statement and its Instructions, the Accounting Practices and Procedures Manual, the Examiners Handbook and by the operations of the Securities Valuation Office and the Non-Admitted Insurers Information Office. Recent developments affecting reinsurance include revisions to Chapter 22 of the Accounting Practices and Procedures Manual, which set new standards for risk transfer in reinsurance transactions and disclosure in Annual Statements of catastrophe exposures and environmental liabilities. (Changes to Chapter 22 are discussed at greater length elsewhere in this book.) Risk based capital, a major development in this area, is of equal concern to insurers and reinsurers but the latest formulas for computing it do not appear to have a severe impact on reinsurers or on the reinsurance programs of ceding insurers.

The accounting profession also is paying increasing attention to standards for analyzing reinsurance transactions. Several years ago, the American Institute of Certified Public Accountants issued an audit guide for reinsurance, which lays out how an audit of reinsurance transactions should be conducted for both ceding and assuming companies. The guide also sets standards for documentation and recordkeeping with respect to reinsurance transactions.

The guidelines were incorporated in the Examiners Handbook of the NAIC. More recently, the accounting profession has become concerned with identifying transactions which appear as reinsurance in form, but which are, in substance, deposit or investment arrangements. This has led the Financial Accounting Standards Board to issue FAS 113, which sets new standards for risk transfer in reinsurance transactions. This subject is discussed in more detail in the chapters on financial reinsurance and insurance regulation.

The actuarial profession also has begun to make greater demands on reinsurers. Actuaries, whose role in the insurance industry has grown enormously in recent years, have the challenging task of establishing proper reserving and pricing for long tail business. Regulatory requirements for certification of loss reserves and reporting of expanded information on loss reserve development have created both the need and the information for a greater actuarial role. Not content with merely having actuaries provide a better understanding of the development of past losses, managements of some reinsurers have drawn actuaries into active involvement in the pricing and underwriting of new business.

Not so long ago, few people outside the insurance industry knew anything about reinsurance. If they thought about it at all, they assumed that all aspects of the reinsurance business were closely regulated by each state's insurance commissioner or that the business was sufficiently competitive so that general oversight of the way business is conducted was all that was needed. However, the attorneys general antitrust action mentioned earlier challenged these assumptions. Enhanced competition is also the goal of federal legislators who seek to repeal the McCarran-Ferguson Act, which provides insurers with a limited exemption from certain federal antitrust laws. Some think legislators see this move as a relatively quick and easy solution to the problems of insurance availability and affordability, which they have been asked to resolve.

The repeal of the McCarran-Ferguson Act would obviously be both quick and simple but its effect would be the opposite of what was intended. The sharing of information, which without the McCarran-Ferguson Act exemption would violate antitrust laws, enables many small- or medium-sized insurers to write types of business for which they would otherwise have insufficient statistical experience to price on their own. Thus, repeal efforts should be coupled with affirmative legislation continuing the right to specified information-sharing and risk-pooling activities. However, even a modified repeal of the McCarran-Ferguson Act could lead to uncertainty and conflicts in legal interpretation which would probably take many years to resolve. Others have suggested that the affordability and availability of coverage would be enhanced by allowing the Federal Trade Commission to play a role in the regulation of insurance.

The establishment of a federal system of insurance regulation has also been suggested as a way to improve the current system. Some advocate jettisoning state regulation totally while others see the federal government working in tandem with the states as is currently done in the overseeing of the banking industry. One form of combined federal and state regulation would have the federal government regulate reinsurance, international insurance and large commercial lines insurers. Proposals including some or all of those elements have been developed by Congressman Dingell, the Reinsurance Association of America and the NAIC. Thus far the federal government has been reluctant to become heavily involved in the regulation of the insurance business.

Changes in Management Philosophy

The governmental actions described above have taken place largely as a response to the rising demands of insurance buyers. Buyers of primary insurance want availability, simplicity, responsiveness on claims and above all, low cost. Ceding insurers want the same things from their reinsurers. But in seeking to provide this for their clients, the management of a reinsurer must guard against "giving away" its capital. To avoid this pitfall and to cope with the cyclical nature of the reinsurance business, there have been basic changes in management philosophy, including a return to the core areas and functions of the business.

Reinsurers also have been exploring new ways of doing business and some entirely new business ventures. They have established reinsurance intermediaries to better compete with brokers, who handle a large share of the total reinsurance premium volume. Reinsurers that formerly concentrated their marketing efforts on direct writing have expanded their role in the brokerage market, even creating separate subsidiaries for this purpose. They also are studying how computers can be used to assist in the underwriting process and to communicate information between ceding and assuming insurers, with a view to enhancing efficiency and flexibility over time. At least one major reinsurer has made a substantial entrance into the derivatives market.

In line with these broad strategies, reinsurers have been seeking to strengthen their technical expertise. While in the past reinsurance companies had limited staff — senior people who dealt with clients and a clerical staff to do the bookkeeping —major reinsurers today employ groups of highly specialized professionals, particularly in the areas of underwriting, claims management, actuarial science and law. In addition, marketing personnel often have a strong background in the technical aspects of the business. Thus, people now moving into key leadership and supervisory roles are likely to be individuals who have moved up the ladder from highly technical areas and who therefore bring considerable technical expertise to these more generalized positions. Other sectors of the financial services industry have gone through a similar shift to senior management with strong technical backgrounds.

Reinsurers have also sought to cement their relationships with ceding insurers by educating them about their responsibilities for handling underwriting and claims functions. Most disputed reinsurance claims are resolved by arbitration and therefore leave no published decisions. However, there is a small but growing body of court decisions, resulting from reinsurance disputes, which emphasize the duties of the ceding insurer. These include the proper underwriting of ceded business, properly advising the reinsurer of developments concerning insured business and proper handling of claims. As mentioned in the chapter on loss development, claims handling includes giving the reinsurer prompt notice of claims so that it can exercise its rights with respect to the handling of these claims and fulfill its obligations to properly reserve for them.

Delay in notifying the reinsurers of claims is a major element in the rising number of reinsurance claims disputes. A primary insurer has a broad duty to investigate claims and, under a liability policy, a duty to defend its insured even when the claims are questionable as to merit or coverage. Normally a reinsurer has no such duties to its ceding insurer. It therefore becomes the obligation of the ceding insurer to make a timely and complete presentation of claims to its reinsurer and the failure to do so may be a basis for a reinsurer's denial of claims.

These changes in management philosophy indicate an end of the period of "innocence" in reinsurance. In the 1970s and early 1980s, it was commonplace to speak of innocent reinsurance capacity. Reinsurers took whatever was offered in the belief that ceding insurers had properly underwritten the business and that they were bringing reinsurers in as equal partners in underwriting for joint profit (or loss). But what appeared initially to be an honest joint venture sometimes turned out differently. As a result, some reinsurers were financially ruined and those lucky enough to survive were poorer but less naive. Similarly, some ceding companies believed that they would somehow be able to collect on their claims regardless of what they did or told their reinsurers. They took on business that they would never have underwritten had they not thought that they could pass on the underwriting risk to others. Such attitudes have led to concerns about the solvency of primary insurers and the collectibility of their reinsurance.

From the age of innocence, the survivors have emerged both stronger and wiser. And despite reinsurers' disproportionate share of society's tragic problems, such as catastrophe and environmental claims, the system has not only survived, but functions well. Reinsurance still performs the basic functions described in the first part of this monograph and there is every reason to expect that it will continue to do so in the future.

7 Constructing a Catastrophe Reinsurance Program

By Peter L. Kamford
Senior Vice President
Guy Carpenter and Company

It took days (and in some cases weeks) for the full and devastating impact of Hurricane Andrew to be recognized. But it only took a few hours for the hurricane to erase the net worth of entire companies as it swept across Southern Florida and into Louisiana. Hurricane Andrew ultimately led to the demise of seven insurers while financially impairing numerous others. Unfortunately for the insurance industry, this disaster was not an isolated event. Over the past five years, 1989-1994, a combination of hurricanes, earthquakes, nor'easters, wildfires and other catastrophes have cost the U.S. property insurance industry more than $32 billion.

How do insurers protect themselves against these natural occurrences to avoid their own financial ruin? The answer, in part, is property catastrophe reinsurance. This chapter will serve as a basic primer on the subject of property catastrophe reinsurance, explaining what it is, why it is purchased and how it is typically structured and underwritten. Some insight will also be provided on the profound changes that have recently taken place in this sector of the U.S. reinsurance industry.

A good place to start is to define what is meant by the word catastrophe. A catastrophe, in insurance terms, is a loss involving multiple policyholders and/or properties and locations. As the name would imply, property catastrophe reinsurance is a product purchased by insurers to protect their property insurance portfolios from losses that emanate from a single common occurrence. Although hurricanes and earthquakes come most readily to mind, other perils such as riots, conflagrations and winter storms are also typically covered by an insurer's property catastrophe reinsurance program. The function of catastrophe reinsurance, therefore, is to indemnify a ceding company (insurer) from an accumulation of losses that stem from one loss occurrence, when those losses exceed a predetermined manageable level.

A Property Catastrophe Reinsurance Program Example

The property catastrophe reinsurance product is structured on an excess-of-loss basis. This means that the ceding company assumes all losses arising from the loss occurrence, up to a prearranged amount (the retention), at which point the property catastrophe reinsurance program will begin to respond. Catastrophe coverage is usually structured so that the ceding company will share or co-participate, albeit for a small percentage, in losses that are greater (in excess) of the retention. To show how a catastrophe reinsurance program might be structured, let's take as an example, a program that might be put together for one of the nation's 20 largest property insurers underwriting property coverages on a nationwide basis. A company of this size might assume at least the first $50 million of losses that arise from a single occurrence. Layers of catastrophe reinsurance would be purchased to cover losses above the $50 million retention. In this example let's say that the reinsurance program has a $200 million catastrophe limit.

The coverage might be structured so that the reinsurance pays 95 cents on the dollar for each dollar of loss, in excess of $50 million. In other words, the ceding company would have a 5 percent co-participation in losses above $50 million.[1]

In a reinsurance program that follows the above example, a $250 million property catastrophe loss incurred by the insurer would be divided between the two parties in the following manner:

Insurer/Reinsurer Participation in a $250 Million Property Catastrophe Loss

Insurer:	$50,000,000	retained net by the insurer
Reinsurer:	$190,000,000	part of $200,000,000 paid by reinsurers
Insurer:	$10,000,000	part of $200,000,000 retained by the insurer
Insurer's Total Gross Loss	=	$ 250,000,000
Insurer's Total Net Loss	=	$ 60,000,000

As this example shows, property catastrophe reinsurance would have provided $190 million in relief to the insurer, reducing its loss by 76 percent. Based on the amount of policyholders' surplus of the company, this reinsurance payment might mean the difference between technical insolvency, or severe financial impairment, and normal operations. For larger companies, a reinsurance recovery under their catastrophe reinsurance program could at the least make a difference in quarterly earnings or dividends paid to shareholders.

In that it serves as a shock absorber for the insurer, a well-designed property catastrophe excess-of-loss program will essentially protect the company's policyholders' surplus and quarterly earnings, and reduce volatility in its financial results. This, in turn, will have a positive influence on capital investors and the insurer's credit rating, and also satisfy regulatory authorities that the company is being managed prudently.

The Underwriter's Perspective

How is property catastrophe reinsurance underwritten by the reinsurer and what do both the buyer and sellers in this transaction have to consider?

In analyzing the needs of the insurer, two primary considerations come into play: the amount of loss that the insurer will retain and the catastrophe reinsurance limit required.

The insurer will establish the level of "manageable" net

retained property catastrophe losses in accordance with its business plan, and the point at which these losses would begin to inflict hardship on the company. The dollar amount of the company's retention will be governed by such factors as the size of the company's policyholders' surplus, the amount of premium income being underwritten, past loss history and geographic exposure to risk together with the likelihood of catastrophe losses.

While the primary company is calculating its reinsurance needs, the reinsurer is assessing the company as a potential client. The reinsurer will expect the insurer to maintain an active interest in the portfolio by monitoring its catastrophe exposures; underwrite in a prudent manner to protect against the eventual catastrophe loss; and assume a meaningful dollar amount of these potential losses in the form of a net retention, subject to the catastrophe program. This helps assure the reinsurer that underwriting discipline will be maintained.

The limits of the catastrophe reinsurance agreement will be influenced by the company's analysis of what its maximum property catastrophe loss could be in given loss scenarios. While it will be the goal of most companies to protect themselves for their worst foreseeable catastrophe loss, this goal will be tempered by price and availability. In some cases, the capacity of the reinsurance market may limit the achievement of this goal.

In analyzing the catastrophe program needs of the reinsured company, both parties will also consider its past catastrophe loss history, the lines of property insurance being covered by the program, the location and construction of the risks being covered and other reinsurance (which would respond first and inure to the catastrophe reinsurer's benefit, that is to say, reduce the loss that will be subject to the catastrophe program).

Once this vast array of information has been evaluated, a catastrophe program structure can be designed and priced. Generally speaking, the catastrophe limit is put together using a layered approach.

Layering optimizes the market capacity at certain price levels. Some reinsurers would prefer that their catastrophe program participations be at a level where the prospect of losses is very remote, while others prefer to participate at a lower level where losses are anticipated with somewhat greater frequency. The reinsurance premium is based on the relative level of attachment — the point at which the particular reinsurance agreement is triggered. In essence, reinsurers judge their risk/reward ratio for underwriting the catastrophe program at various levels of loss.

Using the previously mentioned example, our property catastrophe reinsurance program might be structured according to the following format, with the primary insurer retaining the first $50 million in losses and thereafter sharing losses with the reinsurer on each layer of reinsurance protection.

As shown in the chart below, the reinsurer would pay 95 percent of the first $35 million of the ultimate net loss above the insurer's $50 million retention and the primary company would pay 5 percent. In this example, the co-participation rate stays the same for each layer.

Of course, the relative cost of the first $35 million in catastrophe limit would be proportionately more expensive than the layer of limit above it, and so on, due to the closer proximity to potential losses. In placing this program, the ceding company's objective is to "fully subscribe" each of these layers — in other words, find reinsurers willing to accept its business at every level of risk. Typically, a reinsurance broker will structure and place the catastrophe program.

Reinsurance brokers, also known as reinsurance intermediaries, have knowledge of and access to reinsurers around the world. Frequently, the ability to fully place a catastrophe program will hinge on the reinsurance broker's success in harnessing the global reinsurance market. The art of placing the catastrophe reinsurance program lies in the successful negotiation of the terms and conditions for each layer necessary to attract a full subscription to the program.

Catastrophe Reinsurance Program

Layer	Insurer Share	Reinsurer Share
	$50,000,000	—
$35 million in excess of $50 million	$1,750,000	$33,250,000
$40 million in excess of $85 million	$2,000,000	$38,000,000
$50 million in excess of $125 million	$2,500,000	$47,500,000
$75 million in excess of $175 million	$3,750,000	$71,250,000
Total	$60,000,000	$190,000,000

Explanatory Notes:
Catastrophe protection is generally provided with one full reinstatement of limits per contract term. In effect, the reinsured will have the ability to collect the amounts shown above, two times per layer.

The limits on a catastrophe reinsurance contract differ from those in a homeowners or auto insurance policy. With the typical insurance policy, there are no restrictions on the number of claims that may be filed during the policy period. With some types of commercial insurance and reinsurance policies, there are aggregate limits for the policy period which essentially restrict the number of claims that may be filed. Catastrophe reinsurance claims are not aggregated. Limits apply per "occurrence" or catastrophe, per layer. Once the limit of the layer has been exhausted (twice in contracts that offer one full reinstatement), the primary company will either have an increased retention that includes this exhausted layer or it can seek to purchase additional reinstatements for that layer from reinsurers. Suppose, for example, there are two storms at the beginning of the contract period that each generate $85 million in losses. The primary company in our example then has two options: to continue for the remainder of the contract period with an $85 million catastrophe program retention or to pay for additional reinstatements in excess of its previous $50 million retention, often at a price considerably higher than the original.

In underwriting the catastrophe program, reinsurers will analyze all the information, determining what they perceive to be their expected loss frequency and severity relative to each layer. At the same time, they will determine whether the reinsurance premium is sufficient to achieve the profit margin they desire for offering this protection, after taking full account of their anticipated loss costs and underwriting expenses.

While an academic understanding of the risks associated with a particular catastrophe program is vitally important to the reinsurance underwriter, the supply and pricing of catastrophe protection will also be heavily influenced by current conditions in the marketplace. Regardless of underwriting considerations, if the catastrophe reinsurance marketplace has experienced several consecutive years of profitability, due to low frequency or low severity of catastrophe losses, the market price of catastrophe coverage will tend to decline in response to competitive market pressures. Conversely, frequent and severe catastrophe losses, leading to poor underwriting results (the past five years being an excellent example of this), serve to chase capacity away, decreasing the supply of available coverage with a resultant increase in the price. In other words, the price and availability of catastrophe capacity will follow the basic economic law of supply and demand.

The Catastrophe Reinsurance Marketplace, Post Andrew

Hurricane Andrew brought a sea change to the insurance industry. While Hurricanes Hugo and Iniki, the Loma Prieta earthquake, the Los Angeles riots, the Oakland fire and the great northeast storm, known as Winterstorm Josh, all contributed to the market's recent loss experience, and this affected the pricing of the catastrophe product, no event in the history of reinsurance has ever had a more profound impact on the business than Hurricane Andrew. (See chart.)

Floridians had experienced little in the way of hurricane activity over the previous two decades prior to Hurricane Andrew, although a Florida hurricane has always been viewed by the market as a likely event in any given year. What was wholly unexpected was the sheer size of this loss (at last estimate $15.5 billion in constant dollars) given the location of the storm's impact. The extraordinary dimensions of this event created a situation in which all previous market assumptions concerning the maximum foreseeable loss in Florida were now open to question. Loss models that were previously employed have since been torn down and recalibrated. Despite these reassessments, few market participants would be willing to predict

U.S. Catastrophes Greater Than $1 Billion: 1950 - 1st quarter 1994*

Rank	Year	Catastrophe	Loss (Billions)**
1	1992	Hurricane Andrew	16.26
2	1994	Northridge E.Q.	11.20***
3	1950	Wind	6.578
4	1989	Hurricane Hugo	4.851
5	1965	Hurricane Betsy	4.528
6	1954	Hurricane Hazel	2.934
7	1954	Hurricane Carol	2.797
8	1970	Hurricane Celia	2.14
9	1991	Oakland Fire	1.848
10	1960	Hurricane Donna	1.794
11	1993	Northeast Storm	1.75
12	1992	Hurricane Iniki	1.689
13	1961	Hurricane Carla	1.557
14	1979	Hurricane Frederick	1.515
15	1950	Hurricane	1.473
16	1974	Xenia Tornadoes	1.392
17	1983	Wind, Snow, Freezing	1.323
18	1964	Hurricane Cleo	1.182
19	1962	Wind	1.170
20	1989	Loma Prieta E.Q.	1.149

* Catastrophes include wind, earthquake and fire.
Hurricane Hugo includes losses from Puerto Rico and the U.S. Virgin Islands.

** In inflation-adjusted dollars.

*** As of March 15, 1995.

Sources: Property Claim Services Catastrophe Bulletin and Guy Carpenter and Company, Inc. Adjusted to current dollars using Boeckh Construction Costs Index and Demographic Shift Factor using U.S. Census Population Data.

with any level of confidence the worst loss a severe Florida hurricane could produce. Moreover, confidence in anyone's ability to predict the size of future catastrophe losses has been further eroded by events following the Northridge (California) earthquake, where insured damage, initially estimated at about $2 billion, is now expected to be more than $11 billion.

A significant component of the catastrophe reinsurance market capacity was withdrawn prior to and immediately following Hurricane Andrew, due to the extreme shortage of what is called retrocessional catastrophe capacity. When a reinsurer purchases catastrophe protection to cover the reinsurance it has assumed, this is known as retrocessional protection. A reinsurer would make such a purchase for the same reasons that primary insurers purchase catastrophe reinsurance. The results of retrocessional catastrophe programs during the late 1980s and early 1990s were so volatile that the majority of reinsurers underwriting this class of business withdrew their capacity. Increasingly, reinsurers were now forced to contemplate the underwriting of catastrophe reinsurance on a "net line basis," that is to say, without the benefit of any protection themselves. This dampened the appetite of many reinsurers for underwriting catastrophe reinsurance.

Shortly after Hurricane Andrew and the widespread reductions in catastrophe reinsurance capacity which followed, the capital market sensed opportunities for the remaining reinsurers after others had failed and withdrawn from the marketplace. As a result, a remarkable amount of new capital for underwriting catastrophe reinsurance business was raised during 1993. This amounted, conservatively speaking, to about $4 billion.

Meanwhile, catastrophe market participants have been seeking to quantify and qualify at an increasingly sophisticated level, the nature of the risk that they are assuming. For example, in wind prone areas, geographic exposure data may now be sought at a level of detail never previously captured or even requested. With respect to very large risks located in seismically active areas, some companies are even capturing, for the first time, the actual geographic coordinates so that they can develop data on locations and subsoil composition of the properties included in their portfolios. Hopefully, this will enable them to better estimate the extent of damage anticipated from earthquakes of various intensities on the seismic scale.

The task of tracking all these data is highly dynamic, in that business is either newly underwritten, or renewed or canceled almost every day. This job is difficult enough for the original insurer, but it is even more complex for the catastrophe reinsurer which needs to track the exposures under a multitude of portfolios.

Not surprisingly, the need to capture and analyze these data has given rise to a small but growing industry that can provide engineering and software tools for the task. Recent advancements in risk modeling techniques enable these firms to offer companies specific catastrophe information, such as potential catastrophe loss studies by geographic zone. Insurers and reinsurers may use these products to determine the extent of a company's foreseeable loss in different catastrophe scenarios, based on previous loss data coupled with other damageability factors. Along with these deterministic models are probabilistic models which attempt to gauge loss frequency.

These improvements in estimating potential catastrophe liabilities are a natural outgrowth of the need to reassess maximum potential losses in the wake of Hurricane Andrew and the Northridge earthquake. One might wonder why such techniques were not available before this point in time. In the past, the level of data used for models was much cruder, often based on little more than written premiums broken down by state. When compared with past loss data, these assessments were viewed as reasonable and acceptable, sufficient, at least, for the purposes of catastrophe reinsurers. Since catastrophe programs were being placed successfully prior to 1992, insurers rarely offered more detailed data. But the magnitude of Hurricane Andrew losses changed the rules. Now, if they expect to attract the catastrophe capacity they require, purchasers of catastrophe programs with substantial limits must provide reinsurers with data that include more information and in greater detail, such as their aggregate policy limits in force in a more closely defined area, such as a county or a zip code.

This leads to the topic of where catastrophe reinsurance capacity exists, how much there is, and whether it is enough. While there are reinsurers throughout the world who underwrite property catastrophe reinsurance, the bulk of this capacity currently resides in three distinct markets — the United States, Bermuda and London. In fact, if the $200 million excess of $50 million catastrophe program used in our earlier example were to be placed today, the geographic breakdown of that capacity might be as follows:

United States	20%
Bermuda	40%
London	25%
Continental Europe	10%
Australasia	5%

The above figures are remarkable in that prior to 1993, the amount of Bermuda market catastrophe capacity would not have been sufficient to elicit any mention in this discussion. More than $4 billion in new capital has been raised, predominantly for Bermuda-domiciled reinsurers. The reasons Bermuda is the choice of domicile are numerous but may be roughly categorized as follows:

- Bermuda-domiciled reinsurers can enjoy greater latitude in establishing loss reserves.
- Bermuda's tax system provides companies with a more favorable environment with respect to income taxes.
- Bermuda is politically and socially stable, and it has a well-established, strong insurance community easily accessed by insurers from the United States, United Kingdom and Europe.

Experts now believe that if Hurricane Andrew had hit Miami, the insured losses could have been as high as $40 billion.[2] Based on this estimate, it can be safely assumed that many companies have property insurance portfolios capable of producing $1 billion in losses in a single catastrophe.

Even with the new capacity introduced into the market, it is clear that more capacity is required to meet the demands of some U.S. insurers. A catastrophe program with limits of $200 million to $300 million is far from adequate when the reinsured company may experience losses three to four times higher than that as a result of a single catastrophic event.

Market shortages of any kind generally prompt the development of new products to fill the gap. In the insurance industry, four trends are now visible and likely to continue. Each trend offers a partial solution to the problem of how to adequately protect future insured entities and insurers from catastrophic losses.

The Future — Near Term

1. **Larger commitments from catastrophe reinsurers** — Those reinsurers that are in the business of underwriting catastrophe reinsurance, and have raised capital to do so, will likely continue to increase their "line size" — the amount of reinsurance capacity they will commit — on a given reinsurance program. Several years ago a catastrophe program commitment of $5 million was considered very large. Today many reinsurers will commit $10 million or more and in some circumstances as much as $50 million on a given program. With a demonstrated need for more capacity and the perceived opportunity to achieve a profit, many of these reinsurers are likely to continue expanding their catastrophe reinsurance program commitments.
2. **Continued efforts by insurers to control and quantify exposures** — Larger insurers unable to purchase enough catastrophe reinsurance protection can be expected to maintain their strategy of withdrawing from geographic areas with a major exposure to catastrophes. In some cases, a company's efforts to control its risk exposures will mean no new business will be underwritten in these areas.

   Since demand for the insurance product will increase

with population growth and rising property values, as before, other, perhaps smaller, insurers with more manageable levels of exposure may enter these areas and pick up some of the slack.

In any event, all companies will continue to attempt to quantify their potential catastrophe losses to a degree not seen before Hurricane Andrew. The level of financial and human resources being dedicated to capture exposure data in tandem with attempts at scientific loss modeling will increase, thereby creating opportunity for firms and reinsurance intermediaries with access to expertise in both software and engineering.

3. **Further development of financial market products offering insurers instruments to hedge operating losses.** — In 1992, the Chicago Board of Trade unveiled its catastrophe insurance futures contract, which is designed to provide insurers with a hedge against their property catastrophe losses. Trading volume and acceptance of this product have been slow to develop. However, this and other derivative products still in the design stage ultimately will bring new capital to the discipline of liability management. Acceptance of these financial instruments as appropriate management tools for insurers and reinsurers will ultimately hinge on regulatory approval, but their use should increase once the learning curve has been overcome and insurers become more familiar with them.
4. **Continued state and federal government interest in providing a solution to the insurance crisis** — Faced with withdrawals from the Florida and Hawaii property insurance markets after Hurricanes Andrew and Iniki, state legislatures have had to deal with the public outcry over the lack of insurance availability in some sectors. The potential for future devastating hurricanes or earthquakes and their impact on our economic and social well-being have piqued the interest of both the federal and state governments.

It will take time before any of the government-arranged pools or reinsurance funds can be evaluated and deemed successful. Ultimately, these potential solutions to the availability crisis cannot be judged until they have had the opportunity to respond to the catastrophic losses for which they were created. However, government's interest in the business of catastrophe reinsurance, previously a behind-the-scenes business, is now in full public view.

In conclusion, the challenges to the property insurance and catastrophe reinsurance industry are very clear. For primary insurers, this means that the demands of the public must be met while the catastrophe exposures are managed to achieve long term stability and preserve the company's financial integrity. For catastrophe reinsurers, the challenge is to grow and at the same time meet the demands of their primary insurers, with either new or existing products, or face being a less integral part of their clients' operations.

One thing, however, must be kept in mind. No matter how well-managed the industry becomes, ultimately, nature will continue to hold the upper hand. Only it can dictate when, where, how often and how severe future catastrophes will be.

[1] The co-participation in these losses is generally requested by catastrophe reinsurers as a means of maintaining disciplined loss settlements and adjustments after the net retention has been breached.

[2] "Estimating Catastrophe Losses with Computer Models." *Contingencies*, March/April 1993, Page 45. Estimate based on EQE International Windcap Programs.

8 Financial Reinsurance: New Products for a New Environment

By Bruce A. Bunner
External Director
Zurich Centre Investments Limited
(Holding company of the Centre Reinsurance Companies and Zurich Reinsurance Centre)

What is financial reinsurance and how does it differ from traditional reinsurance?

Reinsurance is generally described as a transaction, where, for a fee, the reinsurer agrees to indemnify a ceding company for all or part of a loss that the ceding company may sustain under the policy or policies it has issued. While financial reinsurance is likewise an indemnification arrangement, it takes into consideration other non-insurance risks such as credit, investment and timing risk — the point at which a claim will be settled and paid. These added risk considerations contribute to the misunderstanding and confusion surrounding the term "financial reinsurance."

Since most reinsurance contracts provide a ceding company with some element of financing, the term "financial reinsurance" is of little descriptive value on its own. Financial reinsurance concepts have changed dramatically over the past 20 years. Early forms of financial reinsurance, such as "loss portfolio" or "time and distance" coverages, applied retrospectively and generally had little or no insurance risk transfer characteristics. The new forms of financial reinsurance are highly sophisticated products, most often apply prospectively, and now transfer varying degrees of both financial and underwriting risk.

Financial reinsurance products are a blend of two disciplines — investment banking and insurance. By integrating the analytical approach of an investment banker with the insurance skills of the underwriter and actuary, financial reinsurers have been able to create a reinsurance agreement that combines the risk transfer benefits of a traditional reinsurance contract with the flexibility found in the new financial products from the banking industry and other segments of the financial services sector.

Response to Change

The development of financial reinsurance can be traced to the convergence of several trends. The first was the growth of liability coverages.

Before the 1970s, the predominant insurance product was property insurance. Because property claims are usually settled very quickly, insurance and reinsurance underwriters gave little thought to timing risk and investment income when establishing pricing models. But in the 1970s, the situation began to change. Casualty insurance emerged as the dominant product, as individuals and businesses sought to protect themselves from the effects of the incipient litigation explosion and judicial activism. And since casualty claims take longer to settle than property claims, sometimes much longer, underwriters could no longer ignore the timing risk. Investment income also became important as the relatively stable interest rate environment of the 1960s gave way to wide fluctuations in rates and sudden rate increases.

Furthermore, double-digit inflation distorted the economic reality of insurers' financial statements, which were based on historical cost accounting. With the shift to casualty products, the symmetry that once existed between the insurance pricing model and the accounting model was partially lost. (As mentioned earlier, unlike property insurance coverage pricing, casualty rates incorporate — either explicitly or implicitly —anticipated investment income.) As part of their strategy to maintain competitiveness, casualty insurers take into account in their pricing the longer duration associated with the settlement of casualty claims. But while anticipated future investment income has been actuarially-assumed in the pricing model, investment income is not considered in the setting of loss reserves. Related loss reserves are recorded under accounting rules at their undiscounted cost. This accounting practice helped set the stage for the development of interest-sensitive, multi-year, financial reinsurance products, which explicitly recognized the time value of money. In a nutshell, insurers saw the accounting rules as an opportunity.

Meanwhile, the volatile economic conditions of the late 1970s and early 1980s had prompted banks and other financial institutions to introduce innovative investment products, such as money market funds, interest-sensitive life insurance policies, adjustable rate mortgages and interest rate futures. Reinsurers borrowed features from these financial products and began to offer various non-traditional reinsurance (and insurance) programs, geared in particular to casualty coverages. Financial reinsurance thus became a logical addition to traditional reinsurance.

In the mid-1980s, there was a dramatic rise in liability losses. The retrocessional market (reinsurers that reinsure reinsurers) was undercapitalized and it was virtually wiped out as escalating losses led to withdrawal from the marketplace and, in some cases, insolvency. Well-established reinsurers also suffered. Pressured by mounting losses from their ceding companies on one side and their inability to collect from their reinsurers on the other, they were forced to raise rates, increase deductibles and withdraw capacity for the more volatile liability coverages, actions that helped to precipitate the liability crisis of the 1980s. The liability crisis, in turn, accelerated the emergence of new products, as creative reinsurers responded to these market dislocations.

The Early Days of Financial Reinsurance

The early generation of financial reinsurance products often took the form of "time and distance" and "loss portfolio" transfer coverages. This kind of reinsurance is known as retroactive reinsurance because it covers past loss events or occurrences.

In a time and distance policy, which carries no timing or even underwriting risk, a reinsurer receives a premium (or a series of premium inflows) from contract inception and agrees to follow a predetermined schedule to pay losses.

Example 1:

Loss Payment Schedule in a Time and Distance Policy

Ceding Company A transfers $100,000 of undiscounted loss reserves to Reinsurer B under a time and distance contract entered into on January 1. A and B expect the losses to be paid within five years. B agrees to reimburse A for losses up to $20,000 annually. With a 5 percent discount rate, the premium amount, before any added profit charge, would be $86,590. Using these assumptions, the expected payment stream would be as follows:

	Interest Income	Actual Loss Payments	Loss Reserves Balance
January 1	$ —	$ —	$86,590
December 31			
Year One	4,330	(20,000)	70,920
Year Two	3,546	(20,000)	54,466
Year Three	2,723	(20,000)	37,189
Year Four	1,859	(20,000)	19,048
Year Five	952	(20,000)	—
	$13,410	$(100,000)	

In this example, B does not assume any timing or underwriting risk. However, if the actual loss payments were less than $100,000, B would earn additional interest income and an underwriting gain to the extent that the losses were less than the contract limit of $100,000.

As explained later in greater detail, time and distance policies, like loss portfolio transfer reinsurance, took accounting advantage of the difference between discounted and undiscounted loss reserves. In the example above, Ceding Company A transfers $100,000 in undiscounted loss liabilities to Reinsurer B but pays only $86,590, the discounted amount, in premiums. As a result of this transaction, Ceding Company A immediately increased its surplus by $13,410 ($100,000 - $86,590), thus bolstering its capital position.

When these coverages were introduced in the United States, they were not regarded favorably by regulators and accountants. Regulators objected to the predetermined payment schedule provisions of such contracts that left the timing risk for the loss payment to the ceding company. As a result, these coverages are no longer recognized as reinsurance products in this country, although they are still utilized to some extent in the London market.

Loss portfolio transfer reinsurance, a retroactive product that transfers the timing risk and (in some applications) the underwriting risk from the ceding company to the reinsurer, thus became a logical alternative to time and distance coverages. Since it transfers all or part of the loss liability of the ceding insurer as of a specific accounting date, it meets the objectives of regulators and accountants. (The reinsurance contract may or may not be subject to a limit on the aggregate amount of losses to be paid by the reinsurer, although a limit is generally found in most financial reinsurance programs.)

Because the principle of the time value of money (i.e., discounting) is often used to derive the reinsurance premium charged for these types of coverages, a key element of loss portfolio transfer reinsurance is the present value financing of past liabilities. Such coverages explicitly take into account the effects of anticipated income on investment that results from the payout pattern associated with the transferred liability. The premium for such coverage is usually a one-time sum paid when the contract is executed. The risk to the reinsurer is that the actual time it takes to settle these liabilities will be shorter than was expected when the reinsurance contract was drawn up. This reduces the anticipated investment income. In instances when the reinsurance provides coverage over and beyond the loss reserves established by the ceding company at contract inception, there exists a further risk to the reinsurer that actual losses may exceed these recorded reserves.

Example 2:

Loss Payment Schedule in Loss Portfolio Transfer Reinsurance

Ceding Company A transfers $100,000 of undiscounted loss reserves to Reinsurer B under a loss portfolio contract entered into on January 1. B agrees to provide A with additional coverage for any potential adverse loss development up to $10,000 or an aggregate loss limit of $110,000. B imposes no pre-determined payment schedule as to the amount of losses that can be paid during any year. Using a 5 percent discount rate, the premium consideration before any added profit charge would be $86,590. If the actual loss payments are 10 percent faster and the total losses develop to the aggregate limit of $110,000, B will lose $11,051 as follows:

	Interest Income	Actual Loss Payments	Loss Reserves Balance
January 1	$ —	$ —	$ 86,590
Year One	4,330	(22,000)	68,920
Year Two	3,446	(22,000)	50,366
Year Three	2,518	(22,000)	30,884
Year Four	1,544	(22,000)	10,428
Year Five	521	(22,000)	(11,051)
	$12,359	$(110,000)	

In this example, B assumes both timing and underwriting risk. In contrast to Example 1, B loses $11,051. This is composed of a timing loss — lost interest of $1,051 ($13,410; see interest income, Example 1, minus $12,359; see Example 2) and an underwriting loss for adverse loss development of $10,000 ($110,000 minus $100,000).

Before the promulgation of recent accounting pronouncements (which are discussed later in this chapter), the ceding insurer in the preceding example could immediately recognize expected future investment income of $13,410 ($100,000 minus $86,590) on the reserves ceded, which added to income and thus increased surplus. This type of reinsurance therefore served as a tool to enhance the statutory surplus of the ceding company. Despite the current accounting disincentives, this kind of reinsurance can still be used to transfer risk associated with a book of business where the ceding company has withdrawn from a particular line of business or jurisdiction, or where the ceding insurer wishes to protect itself from exposure to the potential adverse development of such losses, or both.

The Current Generation

The business of insurance and reinsurance is essentially prospective and, consequently, loss portfolio transfer coverages and adverse loss development coverages have limited applications because they are solely retrospective. Today's sophisticated insurance buyer demands prospective reinsurance products which are tailored to meet the ceding company's specific financial and underwriting needs.

"Finite risk" reinsurance was created in response to these needs. In contrast to the early financial reinsurance products, finite risk reinsurance combines the risk financing element of early forms of financial reinsurance with the transfer of prospective underwriting risk provided by traditional reinsurance coverages. It enables ceding companies to manage the fluctuation inherent in their in-force business which can affect their financial results (the risk-financing aspect). At the same time, the finite risk reinsurance contract provides companies with the means of managing losses in a stable, budgeted manner with a net cost more closely related to actual results than traditional reinsurance coverages.

To fully appreciate when and how finite risk reinsurance can be used to greatest effect, buyers and sellers must understand the interplay between financial risk and insurance risk. The following explains how underwriters view the various components of risk and how the finite risk product addresses some of the limitations characteristic of traditional reinsurance products.

Risk Financing Continuum

If all risk financing activities, including insurance, could be plotted on a continuum, with banking representing the purely financial transaction on the far left and traditional reinsurance representing unlimited risk transfer on the far right, finite risk reinsurance would fall somewhere in the middle. (See Figure 1.)

Figure 1:
Risk Financing Continuum

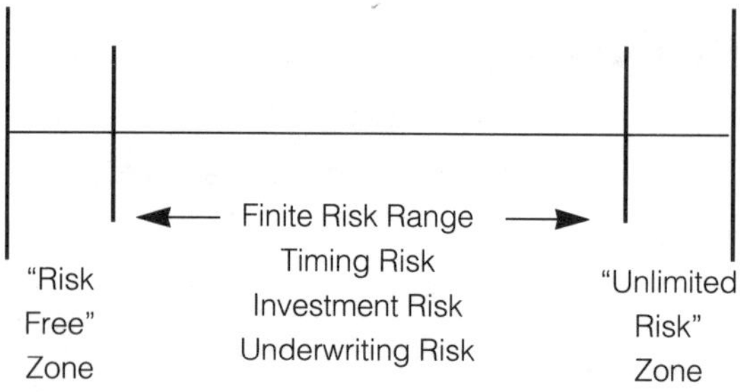

Banking transactions in the left zone of the continuum would be primarily of a deposit-taking nature. The only risk to the "investor" (depositor) is that the bank may not be capable of returning the principal and the stated interest on demand. Since the chance of this happening is slight, the return to the investor for taking this low risk is minimal. Insurance transactions in the right zone of the continuum are most like those in the traditional casualty (re)insurance market. When a premium is paid, the return to the policyholder or, in the case of reinsurance, the ceding company, is uncertain because of the wide range of potential results. The return could be extremely high (i.e., if the policy pays out to its policy limits) or extremely low (i.e., if the policy is not required to respond to any claim). The following example shows the difference in risk. If $100 is invested in a bank deposit account at a rate of 5 percent compounded annually, the investor depositor would receive $105 at the end of the year. On the other hand, with insurance, the same investment — $100 of premiums — could return nothing if no losses occur, or it could return an exponential amount if the reinsurer pays out on claims, a percentage that would be limited only by the terms of the reinsurance contract.

Finite risk coverages, which are located somewhere between these two zones, are composed of varying degrees of insurance risk and financial risk. To the extent that they are skewed toward the left zone, such products have a greater financial element to them. Those that are skewed to the right are more insurance risk-bearing in nature.

Insurance Risk

Insurance risk involves uncertainties surrounding the ultimate amount of any claim payments (underwriting risk) and the timing of the claim payments (timing risk). Figure 2 illustrates the ultimate expected loss as $200, with the premium at time "zero" being $100. In this example, this $100 will grow to $200 with compounded interest by year 10, due to the investment income generated. The band in which the actual loss differs from the expected loss — the variability of results — is the underwriting risk. For example, the band indicated in Figure 2 shows that the loss amount could vary from a low of $100 to a high of $300. The difference in time between the actual date on which the payment is made and the expected payout date is called the timing risk.

Figure 2:
Elements of Risk

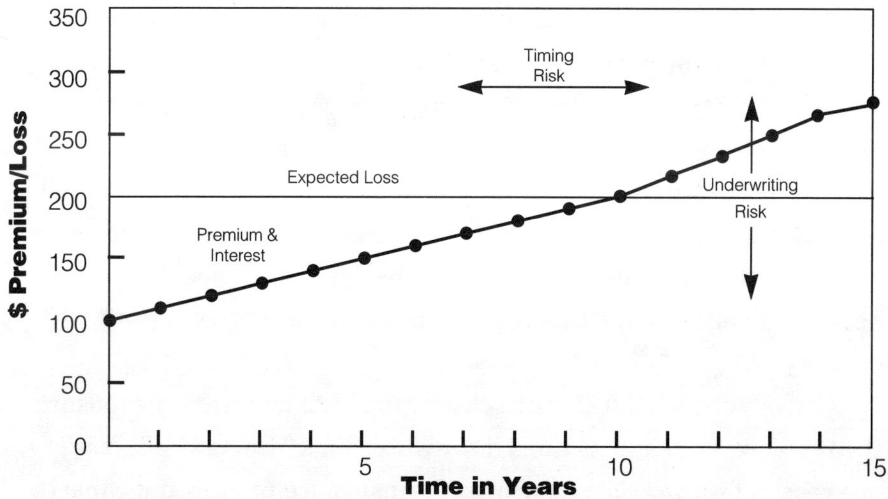

Timing risk can affect reinsurers both adversely and positively, depending on whether the timing variation occurs sooner or later than the expected payout date. In the example, the reinsurer ultimately expects to pay out $200 in year 10. If the payout of the claim is accelerated so that the reinsurer pays the $200 in year 9, then the premium received, plus the investment income generated, will be insufficient to fund the claim payment. On the other hand, if the payout period is extended by one year to year 11, then the reinsurer would make additional investment income and have more than enough funds to pay the claim.

In practice, finite risk reinsurance products usually assume the entire timing risk; however, to cap the underwriting risk, they usually impose annual and/or aggregate limits on the ceding company. This limitation may appear unusually risky to the reasonably risk-averse ceding company but it is not necessarily the case. Ceding companies tend to over-purchase reinsurance coverage because reinsurance contracts are drawn up or reviewed on an annual basis. Finite risk reinsurance is particularly attractive to those companies that do not want or need the unlimited coverage that some excess-of-loss policies offer.

Single vs. Multi-Year Loss Horizons

For all but the most catastrophic of exposures, ceding insurers will generally pay the equivalent of their own losses in the long term, because no reinsurer will pay a ceding insurer's losses indefinitely if it is not earning (or expecting to earn) a profit on such business. To do so would ensure the insolvency of the reinsurer. When the reinsurer becomes aware that it has been undercharging on its book of business, it will either adjust its renewal rates upward or withdraw capacity.

Conversely, when rates are clearly too high for the risk exposure, the reinsurer will adjust rates downward. This "see-saw" effect is one reason for the cyclical nature of reinsurance pricing and capacity. Annual contracts create an environment in which price, coverage and availability can change dramatically from year to year. The multi-year feature of finite risk is designed to address this problem. By committing the reinsurer to both a predetermined premium and guaranteed capacity over a multi-year period, it provides ceding companies with price and cash flow stabilization.

With financial reinsurance, a policy term may stretch from three years to 10 years, or even longer. Once reinsurance buyers realize that the loss exposures to be reinsured typically exist for a period longer than 12 months, they can avoid the cyclical nature of annually-priced reinsurer capacity. Moreover, the process is more actuarially precise when exposures can be priced over longer time horizons, particularly for the more difficult exposures or loss layers where losses tend to be infrequent but very costly.

Profit Sharing

In exchange for imposing a limit on its aggregate liability over the multi-year contract term, the finite risk reinsurer usually offers the ceding company the opportunity to share in the profitability of a contract if losses are less than expected. This profit sharing can take many forms, but the objective is always the same: to minimize the ultimate amount the ceding insurer pays to the reinsurer in excess of its own claims costs.

Under annual reinsurance contracts, the degree to which a ceding company benefits from its own favorable experience tends to be limited, even with loss-sensitive rating plans. For example, it is rare for a ceding insurer to share directly in the reinsurer's investment income. But under multi-year finite risk contracts, profit sharing is the norm. Most include an explicit credit for investment income generated by premium funds held by the reinsurer during the contract period.

Cost and Stability Trade-Off

Figures 3 and 4 illustrate the comparative trade-off between transaction cost and stability under a one-year scenario and a multi-year scenario, respectively.

The lowest transaction cost for risk financing would be no reinsurance at all. The insurer would retain all the risk, i.e., self-insure. But this option is also the least stable and most unpredictable form of risk financing. Traditional reinsurance produces higher transaction costs than self-insurance within any one-year period, but greater stability. Ceding companies thus have to weigh the cost

Figure 3:
Cost vs. Stability Trade-Off (One-Year Scenario)

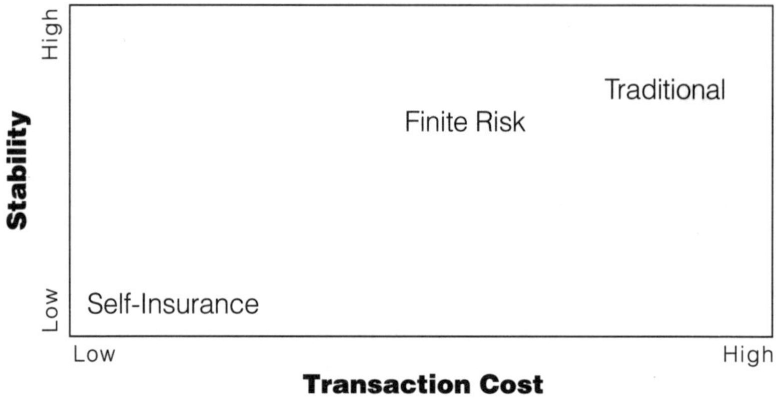

advantages of retaining more risk against the year-to-year volatility created by a larger retention.

Finite risk reinsurance represents a bridge or middle way between retention and traditional reinsurance. It also offers reinsur-

Figure 4:
Cost vs. Stability Trade-Off (Multi-Year Scenario)

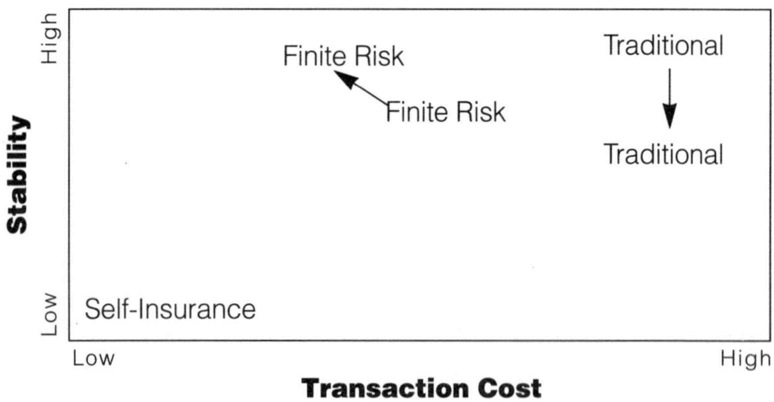

ance at a lower cost for the kind of losses the ceding company would generally be prepared to retain on a long-term basis if it were not for the potential year-to-year volatility of such losses. Finite risk reinsurance is generally less expensive in the long run than traditional reinsurance because of the limited liability imposed by the contract and the profit-sharing provision afforded the ceding company. This shift in transaction cost and stability is illustrated in Figure 4.

The following case shows how finite risk reinsurance solves the problem of balancing relative cost and stability:

Example 3:

Balancing Relative Cost and Stability in Finite Risk Reinsurance

Ceding Company A insures small manufacturers for product liability exposures. Policies sold to the manufacturers provide annual coverage for product liability losses up to $10 million. The ceding company retains the first $5 million of each loss, and reinsures the excess of each loss in the traditional reinsurance marketplace. The ceding insurer has experienced only one loss exceeding $5 million in the last 10 years. The traditional reinsurance market premium quote for $5 million in coverage, excess of $5 million per loss (with no aggregate limitation) is $1.5 million. Ceding Company A wishes to explore whether a finite risk program would produce a more cost-effective reinsurance solution and, at the same time, reasonably protect the stability of its financial statements against potential adverse loss experience.

The following represents a possible finite risk reinsurance approach:

Term	5 years
Annual Premium	$2 million
Coverage	$5 million, excess of $5 million per loss
Term Aggregate Coverage	$20 million
Commutation/Profit Sharing	Return 90 percent of premium less losses, plus interest to Ceding Company A

The benefit to Ceding Company A of purchasing finite risk reinsurance is two-fold. First, Ceding Company A is protected from the possibility of multiple losses in the reinsured layer. Perhaps more importantly, Ceding Company A shares in the benefit of historically favorable loss experience, thus lowering its ultimate net cost. This is how it would work. Under the traditional reinsurance coverage, Ceding Company A's net cost over five years would be $7.5 million ($1.5 million x five years). This figure does not take into account inflation or consider any adjustment of premium rates during the five-year period. Under the finite reinsurance cover (assuming no losses), Ceding Company A's net premium cost after recovery through the profit-sharing/commutation provision would be $1 million ($2 million x five years x 10 percent). Interest credit from the reinsurer would reduce this cost even further.

In return for the stability of pricing and capacity over five years and the significant savings associated with the profit-sharing mechanism, Ceding Company A purchases a finite limit of coverage (i.e., $20 million) over the contract term rather than unlimited coverage each year for five years. Given Ceding Company A's loss history in this instance, the finite limit would be selected to give Ceding Company A the comfort of, and protection against, under-buying coverage, at the same time recognizing that the purchase and repurchase of unlimited coverage over five years may be a costly example of over-buying.

The above example, while simplistic, is typical of the customized approach used by finite reinsurers that takes into consideration the trade-off between cost and stability. However, since finite risk reinsurance represents a customized approach to risk management, to be successful, the reinsurer must adequately define the ceding company's appetite for retaining risk as well as other ancillary financial objectives.

For example, finite risk reinsurance can be used to:

- Smooth the peaks and valleys of underwriting results.
- Lower leverage ratios.
- Manage risk financing more efficiently with respect to investments, cash flow, net income and budgeting.
- Stabilize cash flows from year to year.
- Reduce net reinsurance cost through profit-sharing features.

Regulations

Effective December 15, 1993, the Financial Accounting Standards Board (FASB) enacted Financial Accounting Standard (FAS) No. 113,

Accounting and Reporting for Reinsurance of Short-Duration and Long-Duration Contracts. Shortly after the FASB pronouncement, the Emerging Issues Task Force (EITF) of FASB issued interpretive bulletin EITF 93-6, which further addresses the issue of accounting for multi-year, retrospectively-rated reinsurance contracts. FAS 113 and EITF 93-6 serve as guidelines to prevent abuses of the reinsurance mechanism. In the past, reinsurance has been used to distort a ceding company's generally accepted accounting principles (GAAP) financial position. Most of the guidelines applicable to these pronouncements have now been adopted for statutory accounting purposes.

Initially, the enactment of FAS 113 and EITF 93-6 created concern and uncertainty in the reinsurance market. However, the new regulations have since proven helpful in eliminating the confusion regarding the proper accounting treatment of reinsurance contracts and have actually broadened the spectrum of possible reinsurance applications for which there may be a market demand. The ceding company and the reinsurer must both understand the ramifications of these new accounting pronouncements and the effect that these provisions could have on the ceding company's reinsurance contract objectives, particularly if GAAP or statutory accounting results are materially affected by the contract.

FAS 113

FAS 113 addresses the problem of how to evaluate risk transfer when there is a question about whether reinsurance had been appropriately applied in a given contract situation. Until FAS 113 was released, there existed no definitive rules for determining when a reinsurance product was actually a financing product and when it was, in fact, real reinsurance. To qualify as a reinsurance transaction (i.e., as prepaid reinsurance premiums amortized over the contract period), the terms of the contract must meet the risk transfer criteria as defined by the FASB. If the contract does not pass the risk transfer criteria test, then it is considered to be some other financial instrument, and, as such, is accounted for as a deposit. To qualify for risk transfer, the contract must:

- transfer significant insurance risk (underwriting and timing risk) related to the reinsured portions to the reinsurer; and
- subject the reinsurer to the reasonable possibility of a significant loss from the transaction.

FAS 113 defines risk transfer as "a reasonable probability that the reinsurer can suffer a significant loss." In other words, according to the new regulations, reinsurance requires that the reinsurer put its capital at real risk so that there exists a reasonable chance that the reinsurer will lose a significant amount of money in net present value terms. Evaluation of significant loss hinges on the present value of all estimated cash flows between the ceding company and the reinsurer while considering reasonably possible outcomes.

EITF 93-6

EITF 93-6 clarifies accounting under GAAP for the rights and obligations that emerge pursuant to the retrospective rating provisions of certain multi-year reinsurance contracts as a result of past events. For example, if the retrospective rating provision of a contract is triggered, the ceding company will be required to accrue a liability for any additional consideration payable to the reinsurer for the coverage originally offered that would not have been required in absence of the loss experience under the contract. Likewise, the ceding company will be required to accrue any asset that would be payable by the reinsurer (assuming no future premiums or losses under the contract) based on experience to date under the contract. Additionally, by prescribing the appropriate accounting treatment, EITF 93-6 eliminates uncertainty surrounding profit-sharing treatments contained in reinsurance contracts.

Example 4:

Premium and Experience Account Balances in a Multiple-Year Retrospectively-Rated Contract

Ceding Company A enters into a multiple-year (three-year) retrospectively-rated contract with Reinsurer B on January 1. The contract coverage is $10 million excess $3 million for each and every catastrophic event occurring during the three-year contract term. The initial premium is $2 million but is adjustable each succeeding year, by formula, for an additional premium equal to 20 percent of the deficit, if any, in the experience account. The contract also provides for an automatic reinstatement premium equal to 5.46 percent of the actual loss limit used by Ceding Company A. (In catastrophe reinsurance, when the reinsurer has paid a loss as a result of a catastrophe, the coverage must be reinstated through payment of an additional premium. See chapter on catastrophe reinsurance.)

The experience account includes 88 percent of premiums and 100 percent of incurred ceded losses. The contract can be canceled by A or B as of any calendar year-end with 30 days written notice. Upon cancellation, A receives any positive balance in the experience account and owes B 70 percent of any negative balance. Should B cancel the contract, A has no liability for any negative balance in the experience account.

Given the foregoing assumptions, where an $8 million loss occurs during the first year, the premium and experience account balances are as follows:

	Contractual Cash Reinsurance Premiums	Experience Account*
	(in 000's)	
Balance 1-1-X1		
Year 1 premium	$ 2,000	$ 1,760
Loss ($8,000 - $3,000)		(5,000)
Reinstatement premium	273**	240
Experience account deficit at 12-31-X1		(3,000)
Year 2 premium	2,600***	2,288
Experience account deficit at 12-31-X2		(712)
Year 3 premium	2,142****	1,885
Experience account balance at 12-31-X3		$ 1,173
Total premium	$ 7,015	

* 88 percent of all premiums are included in the experience account.

** 5.46 percent of ceded loss ($8,000 minus $3,000)

***$2,000 + (20 percent of $3,000)

****$2,000 + (20 percent of $712)

Based on the amounts in the foregoing example and by applying EITF 93-6, the reinsurance premium amounts for each year and related balance sheet/liability amounts at the end of each year would be as follows:

	Premiums			Asset (liability) December 31	
Year	Cash Basis	Accrual Basis		Reinsurer B	Ceding Company A
			(in 000's)		
19X1	$2,273	$3,367***		$1,094*	$(1,094)
19X2	2,600	1,648		142**	(142)
19X3	2,142	827		(1,173)	1,173
	7,015	5,842			
19X4	(1,173)	—		—	—
	$5,842	$5,842			

* (20 percent of $3,000) + 20 percent [$3,000 - (88 percent of $600)].

** (20 percent of $712).

*** ($2,000 + $273 + $1,094).

Because the $8 million loss in Example 4 creates additional premium obligations, A is required, as of each reporting date, to accrue the difference between the actual contract cost determined before loss recognition and the cost determined after loss recognition. For example, at December 31, 19X1, the $1,094,000 in assets is composed of $600,000 (which is 20 percent of the $3 million experience account deficit) and $494,000 (which is 20 percent of the projected experience account deficit on December 31, 19X2 of $2,472,000 or $3,000,000 minus 88 percent of $600,000). The base premium payments of $2,000,000 for 19X2 and 19X3 are not taken into consideration because the future premiums are needed to purchase coverage for potential losses occurring in 19X2 and 19X3.

If, on the other hand, no loss had occurred in 19X1, the reinstatement premium for 19X1 would be nil and the experience account would be a positive balance of $1,760,000. Under this scenario, A would accrue an asset for this amount.

New York Regulation 108

In 1984, the New York Insurance Department issued Regulation 108. This provided accounting rules to be applied to loss portfolio transfer coverages in an attempt to discourage abuses of this type of reinsurance. It was quickly accepted as an accounting pronouncement by the National Association of Insurance Commissioners, as well as other regulatory bodies. Under Regulation 108, the ceding company must reflect the loss reserves transferred under a loss portfolio transfer reinsurance contract as a contract liability and the unrealized portion of the gain on the transaction as segregated statutory surplus.

Example 5:

Loss Portfolio Transactions under Regulation 108

Ceding Company A transfers $100,000 of undiscounted loss reserves to Reinsurer B under a loss portfolio contract entered into on January 1 for a premium amount of $86,590. Under Regulation 108, A will report this transaction in its statutory financial statements as follows:

Statutory Balance Sheet

	Before Transaction	After Transaction
Cash and investments	$1,000,000	$ 913,410
Liabilities:		
Loss reserves	$500,000	500,000
Loss portfolio transfer	—	(100,000)
Total liabilities	500,000	400,000
Surplus:		
Segregated surplus —		
Loss portfolio transfer account	—	13,410*
Unassigned surplus	500,000	500,000
Total liabilities and surplus	$1,000,000	$ 913,410

Statutory Statement of Income

	Before Transaction	After Transaction
Premiums	$500,000	$500,000
Loss and Expenses	(475,000)	(475,000)
Underwriting gain	25,000	25,000
Investment Income	60,000	60,000
Other Income —		
Loss portfolio transfer gain	—	13,410*
Net income	$ 85,000	$ 98,410

*($100,000 in loss reserves - $86,590 in premiums)

While loss portfolio transactions still serve certain relevant business purposes, Regulation 108, combined with other GAAP accounting pronouncements (most notably FAS 113), have diminished the attractiveness of such transactions from an accounting standpoint.

Most finite risk reinsurers have adapted to this new accounting environment. In fact, the current accounting environment has acted as a catalyst to accelerate the development of a new generation of finite risk products. The newer products are designed to perform in a manner that places less emphasis on accounting results and more emphasis on economic substance or the net cost associated with the management of insurance risk.

The Future Generation: Insurance Futures and Derivatives

The attributes of insurance risk are essentially no different from other financial risks (i.e., currency, interest, etc.). In other words, despite the differences in accounting treatments for various financial instruments designed to reduce risk, reinsurance is basically a hedge against the uncertainties of insurance risk. In recognition of this hedging concept, insurance futures and derivatives are now being created, particularly with respect to catastrophic events.

Insurance futures and options are now bought and sold at the Chicago Board of Trade. Legislatures in New York, California and Illinois have enacted laws enabling insurers doing business in those states to take advantage of this new form of capacity within the insurance industry.

While it is premature to estimate the full potential of insurance futures, it is not far-fetched to anticipate at some point in time the integration of financial reinsurance concepts with insurance futures concepts. As the industry moves toward the turn of the century, reinsurance as we know it, together with other risk management concepts, will continue to blend and blur. The ultimate beneficiary will be the insuring public.

9 Credit for Reinsurance: An On-Going Regulatory Debate

By Debra J. Hall
Vice President & General Counsel
Reinsurance Association of America

I. Background

The origins of reinsurance are, in all likelihood, as ancient as insurance itself,[1] although reinsurance was not practiced as a separate and distinct business until the 19th century.[2] During the period of economic expansion following World War II, the rising number of reinsurance transactions and the increasing importance of reinsurance to insurers caused insurance regulators and the National Association of Insurance Commissioners (NAIC) to focus directly on this part of the insurance industry.[3] U.S. regulators have been grappling with a number of reinsurance issues ever since, in particular, the standards by which an insurer should be allowed to take credit for reinsurance ceded to an assuming insurer. This article provides an overview of the historical development of some of the key issues, as well as insight into the current status of the credit for reinsurance debate.

A Glimpse Back to 1949

At the 1949 NAIC annual meeting, state insurance commissioners noted that some disturbing abuses of reinsurance had come to the attention of various insurance departments, including abuses of the allowance of credit for non-admitted reinsurance.[4]

The Subcommittee to Study the Question of Reinsurance (Subcommittee) submitted a report to the Executive Committee at the 1950 NAIC meeting, recommending that credit for reinsurance ceded "be based upon the actual value of the reinsurance and the security underlying the collectability and not on the basis of the license of the reinsurer."[5] In furtherance of this concept, the Subcommittee made certain recommendations[6] but no action was taken at that time. The recommendations were still being discussed at the NAIC more than three decades later.

Credit Revisited in 1980s

In 1982, the Illinois Department of Insurance (Illinois Dept.) submitted a report to the Reinsurance Syndicates and Pools and the Anti-Fraud Task Forces in which it advocated steps to curb fraudulent reinsurance practices and promote earlier detection of fraud.[7]

Among the suggestions proposed by the Illinois Dept. was the development of a model law on reinsurance which would create financial standards for assuming reinsurers, accounting for reinsurance transactions and reserve credits, circumstances for prior approval of reinsurance arrangements, required provisions for reinsurance contracts and financial reporting and disclosure of certain reinsurance transactions.[8]

In a subsequent report, *Reinsurance Problems and Solutions: An Illinois Alternative*, the Illinois Dept. made specific proposals for improving reinsurance regulation.[9] The report noted the status of credit for reinsurance at that time:

> Every state permits domestic insurers to take annual statement credits for reinsurance cessions made to "admitted reinsurers." However, state insurance laws and regulations appear to be quite diverse in defining their terms. Illinois statutes, for example,

> permit domestic companies to cede to any insurer, regardless of size, authorized to transact the direct business of insurance in Illinois; conversely, except in rare circumstances, reinsurance credit may not be taken for reinsurance ceded to an unlicensed company regardless of its financial standing... Even those states which only authorize reinsurance credit for cessions made to particular insurers allow credit if the ceding company holds some sort of collateral, such as actual funds or letters of credit, to the extent credit is taken.[10]

As a result of the work of the NAIC task forces, the first model law addressing credit for reinsurance was adopted in June 1984.[11]

II. Current Model Law on Credit for Reinsurance

Historically, the laws governing credit for reinsurance were based upon the concept that credit for reinsurance ceded was allowed when the reinsurer was licensed or provided sufficient collateral.[12]

Over the past 45 years, certain exceptions to that basic concept have been made. Today, under the NAIC's Model Law on Credit for Reinsurance,[13] reinsurance may be treated as an asset on the ceding insurer's financial statement if:

- the reinsurer is licensed in the ceding insurer's state of domicile (licensed)[14]
- the reinsurer is "accredited," that is, in compliance with certain accreditation requirements set forth in the model law[15]
- the reinsurer is licensed in its domiciliary state and that state's credit for reinsurance law is substantially similar to the law in the ceding insurer's domiciliary state and certain other requirements are met (substantially similar),[16] or
- the reinsurer establishes a trust fund in which it secures liabilities of multiple creditors (multiple creditor trusts).[17]

The Credit Model Law treats reinsurers qualifying under the "accredited," "substantially similar" and "multiple creditor trust" provisions in the same manner as if those reinsurers were licensed in the ceding insurer's state of domicile.

Even if cessions to a reinsurer do not qualify for treatment as an asset, credit for reinsurance may still be allowed as a deduction from liability to the extent that the reinsurer collateralizes its obligations to the ceding insurer through letters of credit, trust funds (single creditor trusts), funds withheld or other security acceptable to the commissioner of insurance.[18] A model credit for reinsurance regulation (as distinct from the model law, adopted earlier) was adopted by the NAIC in 1991, which further specifies the requirements necessary for credit purposes.[19]

III. Current Issues

Despite the model law and model regulation, a number of issues related to credit for reinsurance are still controversial. The current disputes among regulators and various segments of the reinsurance industry can be traced back through the decades, some as far back as the 1950s.

Domestic vs. Licensed

There is still considerable disagreement among regulators, and between some regulators and the industry, concerning the extraterritorial application of credit for reinsurance laws. Approximately 13 states[20] have departed from the Credit Model Law and applied their laws, through interpretation or statute, to a licensed company instead of on a domiciliary basis. In other words, a ceding insurer that normally follows the laws of its state of domicile in calculating reinsurance and other credit, must follow different laws if it is licensed in any of these 13 states that have deviated from the model law. The industry has opposed the actions of these states, arguing that ceding insurers will be required to restate annual financial statements on a state-by-state basis, if this practice is allowed to continue. Both the industry and other regulators have charged, in addition, that such actions undercut the NAIC accreditation program and the reliability and effectiveness of state regulation.

Insolvency Clause

The model regulation contains a requirement that, for a ceding insurer to take credit for reinsurance, the reinsurance contract must contain an "insolvency clause."[21] Essentially, an insolvency clause requires that in the event of the insolvency of the ceding insurer, all reinsurance payments due shall be made to the receiver without reduction due to the insolvency of the ceding insurer. In 1989, there was an attempt to draft a model insolvency clause, but the effort was abandoned on account of what appeared to be an irreconcilable difference between regulators in New York and California.

In 1993, receivers entered the insolvency clause debate. As part of its efforts to amend the Insurers Rehabilitation and Liquidation Model Act, an NAIC working group suggested specific insolvency clause language. Instead of recognizing that the provision included in the model law is a requirement for credit purposes only, and that the parties are free to exclude it if no credit is taken for reinsurance, the receivers sought to make the clause a reinsurance contract requirement. They would require that any reinsurance contract not containing the specific language would be construed as if that language *were* a part of the contract. Both industry and regulators have objected to this proposal.[22]

At a meeting of the NAIC in December 1994, there was a compromise and amendments to the Insurers Rehabilitation and Liquidation Model Act were approved. That compromise provides that any reinsurance contract not containing an insolvency clause will be construed to include the prescribed language, regardless of whether the ceding insurer took credit for the reinsurance recoveries. Contracting parties may avoid this result by including their own insolvency clause language in the contract, even in those contracts where no credit for reinsurance recoveries is contemplated.

Lloyd's of London

Pursuant to the multiple creditor trust provisions of the current model law, a ceding insurer is allowed to take credit for reinsurance ceded to Lloyd's as if Lloyd's were a licensed reinsurer. Lloyd's is required to secure its U.S. liabilities in a U.S. financial institution and to maintain a trusteed surplus of $100 million (the "Lloyd's

American Trust Fund" or "LATF").

The LATF consists primarily of premiums payable to an individual "Name"[23] in connection with U.S. business.[24] The liabilities of Names are several — not joint. In other words, one Name is not responsible for the debts of another Name. Only the $100 million of trusteed surplus is held jointly for the benefit of all "policyholders."[25]

In 1993, the Reinsurance Association of America (RAA) advocated a change to the Credit Model Law that would require that all multiple creditor trusts, including Lloyd's, be held on a joint basis.[26] The RAA asserted that a joint trust was necessary to ensure that ceding insurers that take credit for reinsurance ceded to Lloyd's syndicates are adequately collateralized, regardless of the amount of funds that an individual Name maintains in the LATF. Lloyd's opposed this position on the basis that its unique structure would not allow for the funds to be held jointly and because Lloyd's maintains that sufficient security is in place to protect U.S. creditors.

Like many issues in the credit for reinsurance area, this subject has been the focus of debate for decades. In 1950, the Subcommittee of insurance commissioners reported that one of three necessary changes to the law with respect to Lloyd's was the need for

> Some definite provision to be made to assure the availability of assets in the [LATF] for the payment of liabilities in the United States regardless of the individual "Names" to which such funds belong. The method of accounting between the "Names" and the method of reimbursement that might be made in England between the "Names" is a matter of no particular moment to a ceding company that has large claims against certain Lloyd's Underwriters.[27]

The Subcommittee subsequently recommended that the exclusion for Lloyd's with respect to accounting treatment for alien reinsurers be eliminated and that Lloyd's be treated like any other alien reinsurer.[28] In other words, it was determined that Lloyd's should provide collateral to individual ceding insurers to secure its obligations to those entities. This recommendation was approved by the NAIC,[29] but after special hearings were held, the issue was eliminated from the NAIC's agenda in favor of leaving the determination to individual states.[30]

The manner in which ceding insurers should be allowed credit for cessions to Lloyd's has been revisited in the intervening years.[31]

Institute of London Underwriters

In June 1987, the NAIC first discussed the allowance of credit for the Institute of London Underwriters (ILU).[32] It was noted that the ILU had approached the Maryland Department of Insurance with a proposal to accept the ILU member companies, as a group, for credit purposes.[33] Maryland's acceptance of this proposal was viewed by other regulators as a significant departure from the historical approach taken in the Credit Model Law.

In 1989 the Reinsurance Task Force approved an amendment to the Credit Model Law which provided an exception for incorporated insurers under common administration.[34] Like the Lloyd's provision, the ILU was an exception to the longstanding concept that credit be granted for companies that were either licensed or that provided collateral to the ceding insurer.

In 1993, the RAA advocated that the ILU provision of the Credit Model Law, which requires an amount equal to U.S. liabilities plus $100 million of joint trusteed surplus,[35] be amended to require that all funds be held for the joint benefit of all ceding insurers, for the same reason expressed in reference to the LATF established by Lloyd's.[36]

The RAA's suggested amendments with respect to both the Lloyd's and ILU trusts have not been adopted by the NAIC. However, approximately 13 states or U.S. territories have not adopted the ILU trust provision, or, alternatively, have not adopted any of the multiple creditor trust provisions. In those jurisdictions, reinsurers must qualify for credit through other avenues available in those states' laws.

Minimum Capital and Surplus

The amount of surplus that assuming reinsurers, both domestic and alien, should be required to maintain has been a recurring topic of discussion. In June 1984, the NAIC adopted a requirement that reinsurers qualifying under the "substantially similar" provision maintain, at a minimum, the same capital and surplus required of a domestic insurer in the ceding insurer's state of domicile.[37]

In 1988, the Reinsurance Task Force established a working group to consider whether a separate license should be established for reinsurers.[38] The Reinsurance Industry Advisory Committee and the working group concluded that instead of having a separate reinsurance license, an insurer assuming reinsurance liabilities should be required to increase its surplus.[39]

This issue continues to be controversial at the federal level where proposals to regulate the solvency of reinsurers are being discussed. Some reinsurance companies have supported a minimum requirement of $50 million for the assumption of reinsurance by professional reinsurers. Smaller companies writing some reinsurance have opposed even the imposition of a $5 million threshold.[40]

IV. The Focus of Reinsurance Regulation Expanded to the Federal Level

In recent years, the focus of reinsurance regulation has moved to the federal level. In February 1990, the House of Representatives, Committee on Energy and Commerce, Subcommittee on Oversight and Investigations, chaired by Congressman John Dingell (D-MI), released a report, *Failed Promises*, which examined the causes of insurance company failures in the United States.[41] The report noted numerous weaknesses in the state regulatory system and, in particular, identified a number of reinsurance-related abuses.

Following the publication of the report, Chairman Dingell introduced H.R. 4900, followed shortly thereafter by H.R. 1290,[42] which proposed the transfer of regulation of reinsurance from the states to a Federal Commission. Although health care and Superfund reauthorization detoured the Congress during the (103rd) session, Congressman Dingell noted that he intended to introduce a "mini-bill," which would have provided for the federal regulation of reinsurers, surplus lines, industrial insureds and perhaps, the licensing of brokers.[43]

The domestic reinsurance industry has, in large part, supported Congressman Dingell's initiatives in H.R. 1290.[44] Even the NAIC has recognized the need for federal assistance in the area of alien reinsurance. At its meeting in December 1992, the NAIC adopted, in large part as a response to *Failed Promises*, the concept of federal assistance and this was later embodied in the Non-U.S. Insurer Act.[45] It establishes the NAIC or its Non-Admitted Insurers Information Office as the "gatekeeper." A non-U.S. direct insurer would be prohibited from writing business in the United States unless it was approved by the NAIC. Similarly, as a condition of a ceding insurer taking credit for reinsurance, a non-U.S. reinsurer would first have to be approved by the NAIC. The Act sets forth the qualifications of NAIC approval and procedures for the Department of Treasury to act as an oversight authority.[46]

Although the Non-U.S. Insurer Act has not been introduced in Congress, it is likely that it would meet with objections from the domestic reinsurance industry.[47]

V. How Credit for Reinsurance Is Addressed in the Federal Proposals

The Non-U.S. Insurer Act was designed to centralize authority with respect to alien insurers and reinsurers and, at the same time, maintain the current practice with regard to the regulation of domestic insurers and reinsurers. However, the result would be an advantage for alien companies over their domestic counterparts. Alien companies could conceivably have to apply for NAIC approval only once, [48] and this would open the door for the conduct of business nationwide, while domestic companies would continue to be burdened with the present state-by-state system of regulation, which forces them to deal individually with each of the states in which they wish to do business. Unlike the Non-U.S. Insurer Act, H.R. 1290 offered the ability to do business through a single regulatory mechanism to all reinsurers, domestic and alien.

H.R. 1290 provided for the federal certification of professional reinsurers and required a minimum net worth of $50 million, or more, based on the reinsurer's operations, e.g., premium volume, volatility and loss development characteristics.

Under the proposal, a reinsurance department of a primary insurer may assume reinsurance risks by complying with certain standards, including a net worth of $5 million, though the amount of net worth may be increased or decreased based on certain circumstances.

Credit for reinsurance is allowed for a ceding insurer that contracts with a professional reinsurer or a reinsurance department of a primary insurer.

H.R. 1290 provided for multiple creditor trusts, similar to the Credit Model Law. Likewise, insurers ceding to reinsurers not meeting these requirements could obtain credit for reinsurance, as a reduction from liabilities, if the reinsurer funded its obligations in a manner acceptable to the Commission.

In addition to the above requirements, H.R. 1290 imposed a number of other obligations on alien reinsurers, including a provision that the reinsurer file annually with the Commission a translated financial statement, a list of officers and directors, and other biographical information. H.R. 1290 also required alien reinsurers to submit to examination, and to agree to waive any protection provided by its domiciliary country's secrecy laws.

The provisions of the NAIC Non-U.S. Insurer Act reduce the trust fund required of some multiple creditor trusts from $20 million plus an amount for U.S. liabilities, to only $5 million in total — that is, without any funding of U.S. liabilities. The multiple creditor trusts required of Lloyd's and the ILU would remain essentially the same as that required in the Credit Model Law.

VI. The Republican Landslide of 1994

With Republicans winning a historic majority in both Houses of Congress as a result of the November 1994 elections, a radical realignment of chairpersons, coalitions and constituency groups has occurred in Washington. Congressman Dingell no longer chairs the House Energy and Commerce Committee and Republicans are expected to support continued state regulation.

As noted, the non-U.S. Insurer Act was proposed by the NAIC as a result of recognition by state regulators that some federal assistance was needed to adequately address the issue of alien insurers and reinsurers. Several state regulators have advocated the use of interstate compacts instead of federal legislation for this and other regulatory purposes. It is likely that the NAIC and state regulators will continue to debate the merits of the interstate compact approach until interest in federal regulation is renewed.

VII. Conclusion

The debate over a number of substantive issues relating to credit for reinsurance, now at least 45 years old, will likely continue into the future at both the NAIC and individual state levels. The recent federal proposals tend to treat these issues in a manner, which is not substantially different from the Credit Model Law with respect to collateralization. Consequently, debate will continue to focus both on the requirements that must be met before a ceding company can receive credit for reinsurance and the level of government at which those credit-for-reinsurance standards should be established and implemented.

[1] J.S. Butler & R.M. Merkin, *Reinsurance Law* A.2.1-01 (1988 & Supp. 1991). The first reinsurance contract dates back to the year 1370 but the development of reinsurance as it exists today can be credited to the fire insurance business. *National Association of Insurance Commissioners Proceedings, Report to the Sub-Committee to Study the Question of Re-Insurance*, I:475 (1950) [hereinafter *NAIC Proceedings* 1950]

[2] Cologne Reinsurance Company, the first independent reinsurance company, was founded in 1846. The first U.S. reinsurance company was not organized until the

early years of the present century. *NAIC Proceedings* 1950 p.476 and *Insurance Accounting and Statistical Association, Insurance Accounting Fire & Casualty* 85 (2nd Ed. 1965)

[3] J.F. Bank, *The Regulation of Reinsurance, in the State of Insurance Regulation* 128 (American Bar Association 1991)

[4] *NAIC Proceedings* 1950, *supra* note 1, at 49-50

[5] *Id.* at 449

[6] *Id.*

[7] *National Association of Insurance Commissioners Proceedings, Report to the (E5) Reinsurance, Syndicates, and Pools Task Force and (E6) Anti-Fraud Task Force,* I:836 (1983) [Hereinafter *NAIC Proceedings* 1983 Vol. I]

[8] Id. at 837

[9] *National Association of Insurance Commissioners Proceedings, Report of the Reinsurance and Anti-Fraud (E) Task Force, Reinsurance Problems and Solutions,* II:842 (1983) [hereinafter *NAIC Proceedings* 1983, Vol. II]

[10] *Id.*

[11] *National Association of Insurance Commissioners Proceedings, Report of the Reinsurance and Anti-Fraud (E) Task Force,* II:836 (1984) [Hereinafter *NAIC Proceedings* 1984]

[12] *National Association of Insurance Commissioners Proceedings, Report to the Sub-Committee to Study the Question of Re-Insurance*, II:428 (1954) [Hereinafter *NAIC Proceedings* 1954]

[13] *National Association of Insurance Commissioners, Model Law on Credit for Reinsurance*, [Hereinafter *Credit Model Law*], See *National Association of Insurance Commissioners Proceedings, Report of the Reinsurance (E) Task Force*, II:780 (1990).

[14] *Id.* at § 1A

[15] *Id.* at § 1B

[16] *Id.* at § 1C

[17] *Id.* at § 1D

[18] *Id.* at § 2

[19] *National Association of Insurance Commissioners, Credit for Reinsurance Model Regulation*, [Hereinafter *Credit Regulation*], See *National Association of Insurance Commissioners Proceedings Reinsurance Working Group*, IB:926 (1991)

[20] These states include: California, Colorado, Florida, Kentucky, Maryland, Michigan, New Jersey, New York, Pennsylvania, Texas, Utah, Virginia and West Virginia. Some of the laws of these states expressly reference application to licensed insur-

ers while others fail to specifically limit application to domestic insurers.

[21] *Credit Regulation*, *supra* note 19, § 13A

[22] Report of Resource Group to the Model Law on Credit for Reinsurance Working Group in a Letter to Robert Solitro, Deputy Commissioner, New Hampshire Department of Insurance (April 8, 1994). *Minutes of Model Law on Credit for Reinsurance Working Group of the Special Insurance Issues (E) Committee* (May 4, 1994)

[23] Lloyd's of London is an association of individual members who write insurance for their own account and maintain unlimited personal liability to their insureds. A "Name" refers to one class of membership at Lloyd's, an underwriting member. An underwriting member is allowed to write insurance while a nonunderwriting member acts in a brokerage capacity on behalf of the general public and the underwriting members or Names. See R. Mehr, E. Commack, *Principles of Insurance* 46-53 (1960). See also chapter on Lloyd's in this book. In 1994, corporate Names, with limited liability, were admitted to Lloyd's.

[24] *NAIC Proceedings* 1950, *supra* note 1, at 458

[25] *Credit Model Law, supra* note 11, § 1D. The trust deed states that the trust is for the benefit of all "policyholders". U.S. insolvency law has held that ceding insurers are not "policyholders." The trust deed also provides that the rights of all parties are to be governed in accordance with New York law, which raises a question about how the reference to "policyholders" would be determined as it relates to ceding insurers.

[26] Letter from Reinsurance Association of America to Robert Solitro, Deputy Commissioner, New Hampshire Department of Insurance (Nov. 24, 1993) [hereinafter *Solitro Letter*]

[27] *NAIC Proceedings* 1950, *supra* note 1, at 458

[28] *Id.* at 449

[29] See *NAIC Proceedings* 1954, *supra* note 12, at 424

[30] *Id.* at 461-74

[31] See, e.g., *National Association of Insurance Commissioners Proceedings, Report to the (E5) Reinsurance, Syndicates, and Pools Task Force and (E6) Anti-Fraud Task Force, II:893 (1983); National Association of Insurance Commissioners Proceedings, Reinsurance (E) Task Force, Report of Model on Credit for Reinsurance Working Group,* II:727-28 (1989); *National Association of Insurance Commissioners Proceedings, Reinsurance and Anti-Fraud (E) Task Force, Working Group Regarding the Model Law on Credit for Reinsurance*, B:895 (1990) [Hereinafter *NAIC Proceedings* 1990]

[32] *National Association of Insurance Commissioners Proceedings, Report of the Special Insurance Issues (E) Committee*, II:833 and 854 (1987)

[33] *Id.* at 833

[34] *NAIC Proceedings*, 1990, *supra* note 31, at 851 and 891

[35] *Id.* at 855-59

[36] *Solitro Letter*, *supra* note 26

[37] *National Association of Insurance Commissioners Proceedings, Report to Reinsurance and Anti-Fraud (E) Task Force*, II:838 (1984)

[38] *National Association of Insurance Commissioners Proceedings, Report to Reinsurance and Anti-Fraud (E) Task Force*, II:804 (1988)

[39] *Id.* at 808

[40] Discussion of minimum required surplus, 1993: Hearings on H.1290 before the Subcommittee on Commerce, Consumer Protection, and Competitiveness of the House Committee on Energy and Commerce, 103rd Cong., 1st Sess. 286-87 and 298 (1993) (Statement of Lee Bondhus, President and CEO, Reinsurance Assoc. of Minnesota)

[41] Subcommittee on Oversight and Investigations, House Committee on Energy and Commerce, *Failed Promises: Insurance Company Insolvencies*, 101st Cong., 2nd Sess. (Comm. Print 1990)

[42] The Federal Insurance Solvency Act of 1993 was introduced and referred to the House Committee on Energy and Commerce on March 10, 1993. It should be noted that, in addition to addressing reinsurance regulation, the Act also speaks to primary insurance and brokerage issues.

[43] Speech by Congressman John D. Dingell (D-MI) before the 1994 BIPAR General Assembly (May 17, 1994)

[44] Domestic reinsurer's support of the regulation of reinsurance, 1993: Hearings on H.1290 before the Subcommittee on Commerce, Consumer Protection, and Competitiveness of the House Committee on Energy and Commerce, 103rd Cong., 1st Sess. 266 (1993) (Statement of Sandra L. LaFevre, assistant vice president, Reinsurance Assoc. of America)

[45] *National Association of Insurance Commissioners, Report of the Executive (EX) Committee*, IA:136 (1993) [Hereinafter *NAIC Proceedings* 1993]

[46] *Id.* at § 7E

[47] Letter from Reinsurance Association of America to all members of the Committee on Banking, Finance and Urban Affairs of the United States House of Representatives (July 28, 1993)

[48] While some argue that individual states could require additional regulation or regulatory approvals, it is likely that such additional requirements would be pro forma and result, as a substantive matter, in a single license.

10 Alien Reinsurers

By William C. Marcoux
Partner
LeBoeuf, Lamb, Greene & MacRae

The operations and regulation of alien reinsurers have been at the forefront of regulatory debates for the last 10 years. Congressional Committees, National Assoication of Insurance Commissioners (NAIC) Task Forces, individual state legislators and state regulators have all reacted to what they perceive is inadequate control of this market.

This chapter will review the size and structure of the alien reinsurance market and explore U.S. regulation of transactions between U.S. ceding companies and alien reinsurers. This chapter will also consider the valuable role alien reinsurers play in supporting the U.S. insurance market. The chapter concludes with some observations that perhaps the regulatory alarm over this market is misplaced.

What Is the Alien Reinsurance Market?

"Alien" is not the term most entrepreneurs would choose to describe their operations. But, under the parlance of state regulation, "alien reinsurer" is the name given to reinsurers domiciled outside the United States and its territories. "Foreign reinsurers," by contrast, are reinsurers domiciled in a state other than the one asserting regulatory control. "Domestic reinsurers" are those domiciled in the state asserting control.

The phrase "non-U.S. reinsurer" seems more appropriate for our subject matter. It is a term that has recently gained currency and it will be used in this chapter.

Reinsurance is an international business. A list of the leading reinsurers demonstrates that a majority of the largest and most sophisticated reinsurers in the world are non-U.S. reinsurers. They include Munich Re, the largest reinsurer in the world, which is approximately three times the size of the largest U.S. domiciled company, and Swiss Re, the second largest reinsurer in the world. Others include Underwriters at Lloyd's, SCOR Re (France), and Tokyo Marine (Japan). In addition, significant reinsurance companies are based in Bermuda, Scandinavia and Italy.

Non-U.S. reinsurers assume about 30 percent of the premiums ceded by U.S. companies. Some who call for greater regulation of the non-U.S. markets exclaim that more than 1,000 reinsurers from close to 100 countries reinsure U.S. companies. More than 75 percent of the business ceded outside of the United States, however, is written by reinsurers domiciled in Western Europe, Japan and Bermuda. These reinsurers have remarkable solvency records and they operate in markets with strong regulatory and/or commercial discipline.

Non-U.S. markets provide critical reinsurance capacity for U.S. cedents, particularly property catastrophe reinsurance, liability protection (including reinsurance programs for medical, legal and accountant malpractice, directors and officers and errors and omissions coverages), environmental impairment protection and reinsurance for aviation and marine risks. In a number of cases, the non-U.S. markets are the primary or exclusive markets for these reinsurance programs. For other risks, they complement and provide important competition for U.S. reinsurers.

Regulation of Non-U.S. Reinsurers

Non-U.S. reinsurers may underwrite business in the United States on a licensed or unlicensed basis. Because of differences in regulatory requirements, accounting practices and tax considerations, most non-U.S. reinsurers do not become licensed in this country. Some, however, have established licensed U.S. branches or subsidiaries. Licensed U.S. branches or subsidiaries of non-U.S. reinsurers operate on the same basis as U.S. domiciled companies and are subject to the same licensing, reporting and examination requirements.

Recent regulatory action and public debate have not concerned the U.S. licensed branches or subsidiaries of non-U.S. reinsurers. The focus has been on those non-U.S. reinsurers which write U.S. business from their domiciliary jurisdiction, e.g., from Paris, London or Tokyo, and which are not subject to direct oversight by U.S. regulators.

Reinsurance regulation is largely a function of credit for reinsurance laws, i.e., those state laws and regulations which govern when a ceding company may recognize reinsurance recoverables as an asset or reduction from liabilities on its annual financial statement. As discussed in greater detail below, these credit for reinsurance rules have been used to assess the financial strength of reinsurers, to dictate security arrangements and to provide some regulation of the terms and conditions of reinsurance agreements and business practices. To date, however, few laws have tried to prohibit any reinsurance transaction. The general regulatory philosophy has been: You can buy reinsurance from anyone you want, but you can only take annual statement credit for that reinsurance if the reinsurer and the reinsurance agreement meet certain standards. This is a sound policy.

Credit for Reinsurance Laws

In 1984, the NAIC adopted a model law on credit for reinsurance. That law was amended in 1990 and is once again under review by the NAIC. Initially, states were slow to enact the model law, but today it is part of the package of NAIC model laws which a state must have in order to be accredited by the NAIC and almost all states have enacted the model law or have a substantially equivalent law or regulation.

The NAIC model credit law is primarily concerned with the reinsurers' ability to pay. With regard to unlicensed non-U.S. reinsurers, it provides, in pertinent part, that a ceding company can only take credit as a reduction from liability for reinsurance recoverables due from the non-U.S. reinsurer if that reinsurer secures its obligations with funds withheld by the ceding company, cash, letters of credit, trust funds or other security acceptable to the regulators.

If a trust fund is used, the trust must be in an amount equal to the reinsurer's liabilities to U.S. companies plus an additional $20 million. In the case of certain groups of reinsurers, the U.S. trust fund must be in the amount equal to the group's U.S. reinsurance liabilities plus $100 million. The trust fund must be in a "qualified financial institution" (essentially any state or federally chartered financial institution or licensed U.S. branch or agency office of a foreign banking organization) and the reinsurer must report annually to the commissioner information substantially in the form required for the NAIC Annual Statement. By meeting these financial and reporting requirements, the reinsurer can become an approved "trusteed reinsurer."

To date, only a few reinsurers have chosen to become approved trusteed reinsurers, although there is a growing interest in these trusts today. Most non-U.S. reinsurers have chosen the second option of funding their liabilities on a contract-by-contract or cedent-by-cedent basis. Most often the reinsurers provide the cedent with funds held in a trust fund or a clean, irrevocable, unconditional and evergreen (i.e., automatically renewed) letter of credit. The exact forms of these security arrangements are governed by various state insurance department requirements. There is also an NAIC Model Credit for Reinsurance Regulation, which governs security requirements.

Because most ceding companies need to be able to take credit for the reinsurance they cede, credit for reinsurance laws are an effective method of regulating the quality of the reinsurance purchased by U.S. companies. Historically, these laws were primarily intended to ensure that a cedent had adequate guarantees that the reinsurer would meet its obligations. Credit for reinsurance laws have also been used to control indirectly some contract terms. Many state insurance codes, for example, provide that a cedent may not take credit for reinsurance (regardless of the security of the reinsurer) unless the reinsurance contract contains an "insolvency clause," i.e., a clause which states that the reinsurer will pay its obligations without diminution in the event of the insolvency of the ceding insurer. Similarly, state laws often require, as a condition of taking credit for reinsurance, that the reinsurance agreement have an "intermediary clause." This clause provides that the reinsurer assumes the credit risk of any reinsurance intermediary used in the transaction who mishandles premiums or claims payments or becomes bankrupt.

Recently, regulators have expanded the rules governing credit for reinsurance to impose additional controls on reinsurance transactions. The NAIC's 90-day rule for reinsurance recoverables is an example. This rule, which was originally adopted in 1988, requires a cedent to age its reinsurance recoverables and to reduce the annual statement credit taken by 20 percent for those reinsurance recoverables which are more than 90 days past due. In some instances other recoverables may also have to be reduced. Overdue amounts in dispute are also subject to the same 20 percent reduction.

In addition, insurance regulators and the accounting profession have adopted rules to restrict the financial statement, or credit for reinsurance, benefits of "financial reinsurance transactions." In their most objectionable form, these transactions transfer no true risk of loss to the reinsurer. Instead, premium and loss payments are structured so that, in effect, the cedent is able to discount its loss reserves.

The details of the 90-day rule and financial reinsurance rules are beyond the scope of this paper, but it is important to note that these and other new requirements exist. They provide a significant level of control and disclosure regarding reinsurance transactions. These accounting rules, credit for reinsurance laws and contract term requirements apply equally to reinsurance agreements with U.S. reinsurers and non-U.S. reinsurers.

Regulatory Concerns and Responses

Beginning in the mid-1980s, a wave of insolvencies began to sweep across the U.S. insurance industry. From 1980 to 1990, 258 U.S. companies became insolvent. In 1985 alone, there were 45 insolvencies. Some of these were spectacular crashes, such as that of Mission Insurance, and they resulted in shortfalls of hundreds of millions of dollars.

These insolvencies unleashed a number of forces. Many regulators, legislators and industry representatives who were dedicated to strengthening U.S. insurance regulation and enhancing the financial condition of the U.S. insurance industry studied the problems and began to fashion improvements. At the same time, the crisis provided the opportunity for political maneuvering and public posturing by some whose goals were directed towards commercial or political advantage rather than promoting policyholder protection or a strong competitive U.S. insurance market.

One of the areas of greatest concern was the regulation of non-U.S. reinsurers. A now well-known U.S. Congressional Report, *Failed Promises*, published in February 1990 by the Oversight and Investigations Subcommittee of the Energy and Commerce Committee of the U.S. House of Representatives, noted that reinsurance was the "black hole" of insurance regulation. It went on to assert that "[r]einsurance abuse has been a key factor in every insolvency studied by the subcommittee." A sequel to *Failed Promises*, entitled *Wishful Thinking*, was issued by Representative Dingell's Oversight and Investigations Subcommittee in late 1994. It echoes many of the concerns over reinsurance regulation found in *Failed Promises*.

Stimulated by their own concerns, and prodded by the criticisms of Representative John Dingell and other congressional critics, the NAIC began to review its credit for reinsurance laws and other regulatory tools to see what improvements were required. This analysis continues today.

The alarm over reinsurance regulation spread beyond the NAIC. Individual state legislators began to raise questions; even the state attorneys general became involved. The National Association of Attorneys General spent more than two years studying the role and regulation of reinsurers, including non-U.S. reinsurers. Although they expressed concern over what they perceived as inadequate control over reinsurers, they did not pursue any legislative or regulatory remedies.

The primary areas of concern regarding the non-U.S. reinsurers fall into the following categories:

1. Lack of information regarding the financial, management and operational details of the reinsurer.
2. Absence of direct regulatory control over these reinsurers.
3. Adequacy of collateral.
4. Legal rights and remedies in the event of contract breach or illegal conduct.

In response to the perceived regulatory deficiencies and solvency concerns regarding transactions with non-U.S. reinsurers, a number of proposals have been put forth. Some have called for the licensing, certification or registration of all non-U.S. reinsurers as a condition for credit for reinsurance. On the federal side, legislative proposals by Senator Howard Metzenbaum, Representative Dingell and others have, in various forms, required all non-U.S. reinsurers to obtain a federal license or certificate of authority. The requirements have varied but have included disclosure of financial information, the identity of officers and directors and controlling shareholders, and in some instances, submission to examination. The NAIC has at various times also considered some form of review and registration process for non-U.S. reinsurers. Some proposals have included a form of "white list" similar to the list of eligible surplus lines insurers maintained by the NAIC.

Although many international reinsurers would not object to reasonable disclosure or reporting requirements, any move towards the licensing of international reinsurers raises difficult regulatory, political and practical questions.

Reinsurance is an international business and in most jurisdictions it is free of regulatory interference. Regulators throughout the world, including the United States, have traditionally viewed reinsurance transactions as business arrangements between sophisticated parties. The parties to the agreement are expected to pick their partners carefully and to negotiate the terms and conditions of the agreement, including appropriate payment provisions and security arrangements. The United States, with its credit for reinsurance laws, in fact, imposes higher controls on these transactions than most other countries.

It would be misguided public policy for the United States to try to become the regulator of the world's reinsurance market. There are practical impediments, including the costs involved, and any effort to increase the regulatory burdens on non-U.S. reinsurers will conflict with the trade policy of the United States, which is to seek greater trade freedom, including trade in financial services.

Most importantly, the credit for reinsurance laws provide the essential level of control. If a ceding company obtains adequate collateral for the reinsurance obligations, there is much less need to review the financial condition and operations of the assuming reinsurer. The U.S. cedent receives, in effect, its cash up front. As in any commercial transaction, if you are paid in advance, or hold adequate collateral, the financial condition of your trading partner is of much less concern.

Some, perhaps recognizing the difficulties in regulating the international insurance market, have also proposed increasing the security or collateral requirements for reinsurance transactions. Recently, the NAIC and some federal legislators have considered requiring letters of credit to be posted in an amount in excess of the liabilities. Letters of credit equal to 110 or 120 percent of the liabilities have been proposed. The supporting argument, at times presented by domestic reinsurers who compete with non-U.S. reinsurers, is that the ceding company may underestimate its liabilities, and therefore if the reinsurer only provides a letter of credit equal to the liabilities, a shortfall is likely. In response, it has been noted that this potential problem is one of underreserving by the ceding company and the proper reaction is to ensure the adequacy of loss reserves by licensed companies. State regulators and the insurance industry have, in fact, made significant improvements in this regard. In addition, some have called for a trust fund in addition to the individual contract security. The argument has been that in addition to securing the liability reserves, the reinsurer ought to maintain a nominal form of capital or surplus in the United States.

The security arrangements for non-U.S. reinsurers under the NAIC Model Credit for Reinsurance law have worked well. Although *Failed Promises* referred to failures with some letters of credit, there have been few concrete examples of such shortfalls. Most students of the reinsurance industry will acknowledge that letters of credit provide significant security to U.S. ceding companies, certainly greater security than U.S. reinsurers provide to their foreign reinsured companies. The reinsurance failures have most often involved reinsurers who were licensed in the United States or have involved transactions where the ceding company failed to obtain adequate collateral from the non-U.S. reinsurer.

Although the facts indicate that the legal framework for reinsurance regulation in the United States is sound, the uncollectability of reinsurance recoverables has been and continues to be a significant issue for many U.S. insurers. Some of these problems are the result of unscrupulous companies operating from various offshore jurisdictions. Some have used reinsurance transactions to help export funds out of the United States in schemes which were outright fraud. Others have operated without sufficient capital or operate from jurisdictions with laws or customs or practices which prevent meaningful inquiry regarding the financial and management integrity of the reinsurer.

These problems should be addressed. But solutions must be targeted at the problems. Most importantly, in cases of fraud, prosecution is required. This requires a commitment of law enforcement and regulatory resources, which has often been lacking. The insurance fraud provisions contained in the crime bill passed by Congress last year will provide new weapons with which to fight fraud.

Secondly, U.S. regulators, senior company management and investors must insist on more rigorous and diligent efforts by ceding companies in purchasing their reinsurance protections. When necessary, collateral should be obtained for amounts due. If management is not sophisticated enough to arrange its reinsurance protections, then a regulator should not permit it to continue to operate a company.

Finally, greater cooperation and coordination are required between U.S. insurance regulators and law enforcement officials and their counterparts in foreign countries. Movement toward such cooperation and coordination is already underway.

Significant new requirements for all non-U.S. reinsurers, however, are not necessary. They will only burden the legitimate reinsurers. The fraudsters will violate the new laws, just as eagerly as they did the old laws.

Conclusion

Non-U.S. reinsurers provide vital capacity for the U.S. insurance market and healthy competition to the U.S. domestic reinsurers. As discussed above, reinsurance transactions with non-U.S. reinsurers are subject to significant and effective regulation. The NAIC Model Law on Credit for Reinsurance and various accounting rules require significant disclosure of the amount and nature of reinsurance ceded abroad, dictate cash or its equivalent be held as collateral for the obligations and provide regulators, as well as cedents, with ample opportunity to ensure the contract obligations will be performed.

Improvements can be made. Most importantly, cedents should use greater diligence in choosing their reinsurers (whether domestic or non-U.S.), and there should be more effective regulatory audits of ceding companies to ensure that they are complying with the current legal standards.

Reinsurance, in general, and non-U.S. or alien reinsurance, in particular, are a mystery to most legislators and many regulators. There is a danger that a fear of the unknown can create an overreaction which will harm U.S. companies. Although some problems regarding the regulation of the reinsurance market remain, the cure requires fine tuning, not a massive overhaul or substantial increase in standards.

11 The Growth of Reinsurance Regulation

By Norris W. Clark, CFE
Deputy Commissioner, Financial Surveillance and
Ramon M. Calderon, CFE
Chief Examiner
California Insurance Department

Since the late 1980s, regulatory oversight of reinsurance has increased by almost geometric proportions. This expansion has come in three separate, but related, areas: (1) disclosure; (2) assessment of risk transfer and accounting; and (3) security.

In 1988, accounting requirements for reinsurers were minimal. The requirements included in the *National Association of Insurance Commissioners Accounting Practices and Procedures Manual* (NAIC-APPM) were dealt with in the space of two or three pages. In addition, there was little information on the amount of reinsurance that could be recovered from authorized or unauthorized reinsurers. The disclosures required at that time were covered in just four parts of Schedule F of the NAIC Annual Statement Blank and the NAIC had not even considered the concept of risk-based capital.

What then precipitated the concerns that have propelled reinsurance regulation to its current level? Several factors, among them the importance of reinsurance to primary insurers' financial well-being.

One need only look at the degree to which insurers rely on reinsurance to understand why regulators might want to scrutinize what is going on in this area. In 1992, the last year for which data are available, insurers ceded over $49 billion of their premiums to reinsurers. Reinsurance recoverables on paid losses and loss adjustment expenses (LAE) were approximately $10 billion, and reinsurance recoverables on unpaid losses and LAE were approximately $115 billion.[1] When those figures are looked at in conjunction with the property/casualty industry's policyholder surplus of $175 billion (as of year-end 1992), it is not difficult to see the extent to which the solvency of primary companies depends on their ability to collect on their reinsurance contracts.

Another factor contributing to the pressure on state regulators to heighten their regulation of reinsurance is the growing interest of the federal government in this area of regulation. The failures of several well-known large property/casualty insurers in the mid-1980s, caused, in large part, by the inability of those companies to recover reinsurance from their reinsurers, initially prompted federal officials to investigate how the states regulated reinsurers. After huge losses in the early 1990s there was widespread fear that even the most venerable of insurance institutions, Lloyd's of London, might ultimately have trouble honoring its obligations.

Yet another factor was the evolving nature of financial reinsurance. While almost all reinsurance involves some elements of financing, during the 1980s new forms of financing appeared under the guise of reinsurance. The first forms of financial reinsurance provided for virtually no insurance risk transfer and were essentially crude forms of loss reserve discounting (e.g., retroactive loss portfolio transfers with loss payment schedules). See the chapter on financial reinsurance. However, later agreements of this type were less and less transparent, making it much more difficult for regulators to determine whether any significant insurance risk transfer was occurring.

What problems did this present to regulators? A financially troubled insurer's deteriorating condition might be masked by so-called reinsurance which was primarily providing temporary financing — not a significant sharing or transfer of risk —thus, precluding timely regulatory intervention and corrective action.

Regulators are not the only group active in this area. In the last few years, the Financial Accounting Standards Board (FASB) has tightened significantly generally accepted accounting principles (GAAP) for reinsurance transactions. Its pronouncements culminated with the Statement of Financial Accounting Standards No. 113 (FAS 113), the most extensive accounting standard developed to date on reinsurance transactions. Because the comprehensiveness of that standard was so much greater than the existing statutory guidance provided in Chapter 22 of the NAIC-APPM, the NAIC was compelled either to adopt FAS 113 or to develop new accounting guidance for reinsurance. The NAIC chose the latter approach and adopted a completely revised and more comprehensive Chapter 22.

1. Disclosure

Schedule F of the NAIC Annual Statement has always been the key document for detailed disclosure of reinsurance. It is in Schedule F that information on all insurance business ceded and assumed by an insurer can be found. Until recently, Schedule F had generally changed in an evolutionary manner, with a few new refinements almost every year. From adding a column for reporting incurred but not reported (IBNR) ceded losses in 1984, to information regarding the age of reinsurance recoverables on paid losses (which led to a penalty provision for authorized reinsurance in 1988), Schedule F was expanded slowly but steadily. In 1992, evolutionary change gave way to revolutionary change when the NAIC adopted a new and expanded Schedule F for the 1993 Annual Statement Blank.

The new Schedule F contains eight parts. Part 1 is Assumed Reinsurance and replaces the old Part 1A-Section 2. Whereas the old assumed reinsurance schedule basically required only financial data on reinsurance payable on paid and unpaid losses to each reinsured, the new Part 1 requires much more detail. The insurer must report (for each reinsured) reinsurance on paid losses and loss adjustment expenses (LAE), known case losses (reported reserves) and LAE, IBNR losses and LAE, bulk IBNR losses (to make up for any deficit in IBNR reserves), contingent commission payable, assumed premium receivable, funds held or on deposit, letters of credit posted and amounts of assets pledged or compensating balances.

Schedule F-Part 2 is the old Part 1B and is unchanged. This part requires information on premiums ceded or assumed for portfolio reinsurance effected or cancelled during the calendar year.

Schedule F-Parts 3 and 4 replace the old Part 1A-Section 1. While the old Part 1A-Section 1 required that financial data on ceded reinsurance be reported in nine columns, the level of detail required by the new Parts 3 and 4 extends to 18 columns and includes greatly expanded information. To illustrate the increased detail, reinsurance recoverable on paid and unpaid losses and LAE (two columns in the old Part 1A-Section 1) have now become reinsurance recoverable on paid losses, paid LAE, paid known case losses, known case LAE, IBNR losses, and IBNR LAE (six columns). Part 3 also requires new information not previously required, such as ceded balances payable and other amounts due to reinsurers. Part 4 is a more extensive aging schedule of reinsurance recoverables than was included in the old Part 1A-Section 1 and incorporates calculations of the percentages of total recoverables overdue and overdue more than 120 days. (For comparison purposes, old Part 1A-Section 1 is shown in Exhibit 1 and new Parts 3 and 4 are Exhibits 2 and 3 at the end of this chapter).

Schedule F-Part 5 basically replaces old Part 2A-Sections 1 and 2 and covers unauthorized reinsurance and penalties for unauthorized reinsurance. The old Part 2A-Section 1 required more detailed information on loss recoverables from unauthorized reinsurers because that detail was not required in the old Part 1A-Section 1. Now, since that loss recoverable information is reported in even more detail in the new Part 3, the emphasis of this new Part 5 is on information relative to overdue amounts and amounts in dispute, and the calculation of the statutory surplus penalty.[2]

Schedule F-Parts 6 and 7 basically replace old Schedule F-Part 2B-Sections 1 and 2 and cover overdue penalties for authorized reinsurance. As with the new Part 5, since detailed recoverable reinsurance information is now included in Part 3, these two new parts now provide more information on amounts in dispute and the calculation of the statutory surplus penalty.

Finally, Schedule F-Part 8 is the old Part 1 and is a restatement of the balance sheet to identify net credit for ceded reinsurance. The reason for Part 8 is essentially to gross up the balance sheet to provide a snapshot of the extent to which an insurer is relying on its reinsurers.

After reading through all eight parts of Schedule F, an obvious question arises. Why all this detail? The intent was to allow insurance regulators to do a much more extensive analysis of a company's reinsurance programs and its exposure to additional risk should any of its reinsurers fail to live up to its contractual obligations. Certainly such analysis could have been done before the advent of the new Schedule F. However, it would have required extensive work by the company or by an insurance department's examiners (or analysts) to compile the data in the format now required in the new Schedule F or in another similar format. The fact that all companies now compile data in the prescribed format is expected to increase the effectiveness of reinsurance analysis as well as expedite it.

2. Assessment of Risk Transfer and Accounting

The Property-Casualty Reinsurance Study Group of the NAIC's Accounting Practices and Procedures Task Force significantly modified the existing statutory accounting guidance set out in Chapter 22 of the Accounting Practices and Procedures Manual. The changes to Chapter 22 are largely based on FAS 113. However, Chapter 22 differs from FAS 113 by retaining loss portfolio accounting, the netting of loss reserves against reinsurance, immediate recognition of ceded reinsurance commissions, and the effective date of accounting implementation.

Reinsurance and Transfer of Risk

Chapter 22 identifies the essential ingredient of a reinsurance contract as the shifting or transfer of insurance risk. It is this element — insurance risk transfer — that allows a reinsurance contract to qualify on the financial statement for loss reserve credit. Until recently, the term transfer of risk had varied meanings and applications. Chapter 22 has now defined transfer of insurance risk as uncertainties about how much the reinsurer will ultimately pay and when it will be paid.[3] Chapter 22 goes on to state that investment risk is not an element of insurance risk. These definitions parallel those of FAS 113.

The determination of whether or not a reinsurance contract contains the appropriate transfer of insurance risk requires a comprehensive understanding of the reinsurance contract between the ceding company and reinsurer, and of other reinsurance contracts, if they are related to the contract in question. Arguably, in order to arrive at a comprehensive understanding of the reinsurance contract, one must evaluate those contractual features which have the effect of limiting the amount of risk to the reinsurer, or delaying the reimbursement of claims by the reinsurer.[4] Contractual provisions which may have the effect of limiting risk to the reinsurer include refunds based on favorable claims experience, cancellation provisions, or the addition of more profitable lines of business to the reinsurance contract. Contractual provisions which have the effect of delaying reimbursement of claims by the reinsurer include payment schedules and accumulating retentions from multiple years[5].

As in FAS 113, the indemnification of the ceding company by the reinsurer, against loss or liability relating to insurance risk, requires that the reinsurer assume significant risk[6] and that there is a reasonable possibility that the reinsurer may realize a significant loss from the transaction.

Significant insurance risk is not considered to have been assumed if the probability of a significant variation in either the amount or the timing of payments by the reinsurer is remote, as was the case in early financial reinsurance contracts. Chapter 22 additionally states that this insurance risk transfer requirement is met only when both the amount and timing of the reinsurer's payments depend on, and vary directly with, the amount and timing of claims settled by the ceding company. The intent here is that once the reinsurer's participation is triggered, it should reimburse the ceding company for claims as soon as the ceding company has paid its claimants.

The measurement of significant loss potential is evaluated by comparing the present value of all cash flows with the present value of the amounts paid, or deemed to have been paid, to the reinsurer. If the reinsurer is not exposed to the reasonable possibility of significant loss based on the cash flow analyses, the ceding company will be considered indemnified only if the reinsurer has assumed substantially all of the insurance risk relating to the reinsured portions of the underlying insurance contracts. Under such a scenario, the ceding company would have ceded all or almost all of the risk it had assumed in issuing insurance policies. Thus the reinsurer's exposure would be basically the same as the direct insurer's exposure. Apart from the analyses of cash flows associated with such reinsurance, there are other considerations. For example, contractual provisions that delay timely reimbursement to the ceding company would violate the conditions necessary for transfer of insurance risk.

In evaluating contractual provisions which establish the transfer of significant insurance risk, Chapter 22 stresses substance over form and cautions the reader to look at the intent of contractual provisions such as payment schedules and accumulating retentions from multiple years.

Accounting for Reinsurance

In both FAS 113 and Chapter 22, accounting for reinsurance largely depends on whether the contract is considered prospective or retroactive. The distinction between both forms of reinsurance is based on whether the contract reinsures future (prospective) or past (retroactive) insured events covered by the underlying insurance policies. For those prospective reinsurance contracts which meet the conditions for transfer of insurance risk, reinsurance premiums ceded are reported as a reduction to written and earned premiums by the ceding company, and are earned over the remaining contract period in proportion to the amount of reinsurance protection provided. Reinsurance recoverables on paid losses are reported as an asset on the balance sheet. While FAS 113 requires the grossing up of reinsurance recoverables and unpaid loss reserves for purposes of financial statement presentation, Chapter 22 continues to net reinsurance recoverables against gross loss reserves.

Due to past abuses of "surplus relief" reinsurance and the resulting distortion of underwriting results, Chapter 22 devotes much attention to the accounting treatment of retroactive reinsurance contracts. It essentially preserves the favorable accounting treatment previously afforded "loss portfolio" reinsurance contracts by allowing an immediate surplus gain. However, the contract must meet certain conditions. Prerequisites for such accounting treatment are many and they require a strict interpretation of the contractual provisions. Basically, to be acceptable, these retroactive contracts must meet the following requirements:

- Include an acceptable insolvency clause.[7]
- Prohibit cancellation of the agreement without approval of the insurance commissioner of the domiciliary state of the ceding company.
- Provide for prompt payment of recoveries due the ceding company for payment of losses and claim obligations incurred.
- Ensure that the reinsurance agreement constitutes the entire agreement between the parties and does not contain profit guarantees.
- Ensure that the reinsurance agreement provides for reports of premiums and losses no less frequently than each quarter.
- Ensure that the consideration paid by the ceding company is a "sum certain" and is stated as such in the agreement.[8]

Insurers with ceded business under retroactive contracts that meet the conditions stated above must fully disclose the transaction in the annual and interim financial statements. In addition, the ceding company must:

- Record the total amount of all retroactive reinsurance as a write-in item on page 3, and record it as a reduction in liability.
- Record its loss and loss expense reserves on a gross basis on its balance sheet (without recognition of the retroactive reinsurance) and in all schedules and exhibits, likewise for the assuming company.
- Segregate surplus resulting from any retroactive reinsurance as a "special surplus fund" and classify it as "retroactive reinsurance account."
- Report the amount of the gain from the transaction as a write-in item "retroactive reinsurance gain" as a part of Other Income in the Underwriting and Investment Exhibit. (The surplus gain may not be considered earned surplus until such time as the underlying claim obligations transferred have been extinguished.[9])

In the event that a reinsurance contract does not contain both elements of insurance risk (amount of loss payments and timing of loss payments), the reinsurance contract balances must be accounted for and reported as deposits in the NAIC annual and interim financial statements, as follows:

- At the outset of the reinsurance contract, the net ceded premium is recorded as a deposit (asset) on the ceding company's books and as a liability on the assuming company's books.[10]
- No deduction is made from the loss and LAE reserves on the ceding company's balance sheet, schedules and exhibits.[11]

The accounting requirements listed above are not applicable to retroactive reinsurance transactions which are part of a court-ordered rehabilitation, liquidation or receivership; structured settlement annuities for individual claims purchased to implement settlements of policy obligations; intercompany reinsurance agreements among companies 100 percent owned by a common parent (provided there is no surplus gain); and the termination or reduction in participation in reinsurance treaties entered into in the ordinary course of business.

In summary, the new Chapter 22 provides a more definitive framework by which to evaluate reinsurance transactions, and results in more consistency in the accounting treatment of reinsurance. With the seemingly endless availability of creative reinsurance contracts in the marketplace, Chapter 22 enables the regulator to effectively curb the misuse of reinsurance contracts by means of financial reinsurance accounting and not mere prohibition or other regulatory constraint. Although professional judgment remains a factor in evaluating terms, such as "reasonably possible" and "significant insurance risk," the strength of Chapter 22 is in its recognition of substance of transaction over form.

Security

An important part of reinsurance regulation is security. This is addressed in the law that covers credit for reinsurance. The NAIC Model Law, which was originally adopted by the NAIC in 1984 and which is covered in another chapter of this book, was last amended in 1990 and is currently undergoing yet further amendment. Suffice it to say that the model law and the laws of most states which are similar or related to the model law, are the keystones for regulating the security of reinsurance. If security is not deemed to exist under the law (i.e., the reinsurer is not authorized or accredited, and the reinsurance from an unauthorized reinsurer is not secured by funds withheld, trust funds or letters of credit), then a credit for reinsurance against loss reserves is not allowed. For the ceding company, unsecured reinsurance results in a charge against surplus.

It was previously noted that Schedule F also has penalties for potentially uncollectible reinsurance, such penalties being calculated on the aging of reinsurance recoverables. That penalty is also a charge to a ceding insurer's surplus.

Now, another element has been added which provides an additional tool for the regulation of reinsurance security. That element is the credit risk charge which is included in the Property/Casualty Risk Based Capital ("RBC") formula. All of the charges in the RBC formula, including the credit risk charge, require an insurer to provide additional capital to support the risks associated with doing insurance business; thus, security for reinsurance should be enhanced by RBC.

Credit risk is defined as the risk of default on amounts due from reinsurers, policyholders, or other creditors, and is one of the four categories of risks considered in the RBC formula.[12]

Specifically, the factor for reinsurance recoverables [paid and unpaid (Schedule F - Part 3) less any applicable reinsurance penalty (from Schedule F, Part 7 and included in Page 3, Line 13)] is 10 percent. The following types of cessions are exempt from this charge:

- Cessions to state mandated involuntary pools and associations or to federal insurance programs.
- Cessions to voluntary market mechanism pools and associations.
- Cessions to U.S. affiliates, subsidiaries, and parents.

Voluntary market mechanism pools and associations are those:

- Which have been established to provide a special voluntary mechanism for coverages such as aircraft, flood, hail, industrial, nuclear, railroad transportation, workers compensation, etc.;
- Where the recoverability of amounts ceded to the pool by the direct writer or servicing carrier is assured by the facility; and
- Where the pool or association participants number 10 or more and such participants share proportionately in the experience of the pool or association.[13]

As noted above, the credit risk charge for reinsurance ceded is 10 percent; however, that factor is attenuated when subjected to the covariance adjustment in the RBC formula. The covariance adjustment in the formula is intended to reflect the presumption that the various risks accounted for in the formula are generally independent, i.e., adverse experience in all of the risk categories will not occur simultaneously. To mathematically adjust for this independence of risk, the square root of the sum of the squares of the various risk charges is calculated. In the case of the credit risk charge, the NAIC Working Group that developed the RBC formula felt that credit risk might not be totally independent of the loss and LAE risk charge.[14] Therefore 50 percent of the total credit charge is added to the loss and LAE charge and the remaining 50 percent is treated as an independent factor before those charges are subjected to the covariance adjustment.

Conclusion

Over the last 10 years, insurance regulators and the NAIC have systematically and aggressively addressed the previous weaknesses of reinsurance regulation. Lax regulation of reinsurance was one of the factors that contributed to the insolvencies of several insurance companies, with the resultant hardships to policyholders. Those insolvencies led to criticism of the regulatory process from several camps, most notably the federal government (e.g., Congressman Dingell and the General Accounting Office). But more importantly, the insolvencies and the fallout from them provided the badly needed impetus to thoroughly examine and rethink the state of reinsurance regulation. While it took a little while to develop momentum, the changes made over the last four years have been astonishing.

The comprehensive scheme of regulation which has been summarized in this chapter is indicative of the extraordinary efforts made by regulators and the NAIC in this very important area. The focus of these efforts was broad and the results are the requirements for extensive disclosure of reinsurance activities in the annual financial statement, well thought out and detailed guidance for the evaluation of risk transfer and accounting, and improved and new regulatory tools to assure that security for reinsurance is available (and if not, appropriately charging a ceding company's surplus for the lack of security).

Is the regulator's work with respect to reinsurance now complete? Certainly not. Since the insurance environment is dynamic, additional refinements in the regulatory scheme are more than likely. However the changes will not be of the magnitude of those implemented during the early 1990s. Meanwhile, regulators will take advantage of the tools that they already have — new fuller disclosure, more complete accounting and stricter security, which will enhance solvency regulation and protection of policyholders.

[1] NAIC Statistical Compilation - 1992, National Association of Insurance Commissioners, Kansas City, MO.

[2] In 1989, a statutory surplus penalty for potentially uncollectible reinsurance from authorized reinsurers was developed by the NAIC Property/Casualty Reinsurance Study Group. That penalty calculation was subsequently also required for unauthorized reinsurers.

If an insurer has recoverables from a reinsurer more than 90 days past due, it must determine whether a surplus penalty is to be imposed and, if so, how large. Reinsurance recoverable from a reinsurer that has not paid under the terms of its contract would be shown in two different ways, depending on the ratio of amounts past due to the total amount recoverable from that reinsurer together with the amounts received from it within the past 90 days. If the ratio of amounts over 90 days past due (excluding amounts in dispute) divided by the total reinsurance recoverable from that reinsurer on paid losses (excluding amounts in dispute) and amounts received in the past 90 days, is less than 20 percent, the amount over 90 days past due (excluding amounts in dispute) would be in a column for reinsurers showing a ratio of less than 20 percent past due reinsurance recoverable. If the ratio is 20 percent or greater, the potential effect and implications would be more serious. In such a case, all recoverables due from that reinsurer (including unearned premiums, paid and unpaid losses, paid and unpaid allocated loss adjustment expenses and IBNR) would be shown on new Schedule F-Part 7.

(James M. Shamberger, "Recent Annual Statement Changes: Improved Reinsurance Data", *Reinsurance: Fundamentals and New Challenges*, I.I.I., 1989, p.96)

[3] *NAIC Accounting Practices and Procedures Manual for Property/Casualty Insurance Companies*, 10/94, p.22-1

[4] *Ibid.*, p.22-2

[5] Aggregate retentions were typically and historically calculated on a calendar year basis, while accumulating retention provisions and calculations were found on multiple year contracts. A typical ceding insurer aggregate retention might be a "loss

ratio of 75 percent for calendar year 1994," but an accumulating retention would be a "75 percent loss ratio times net earned premium over the term of the reinsurance contract." The problem with an accumulating retention can be illustrated by this hypothetical:

For simplicity, assume level premium volume subject to the reinsurance for both years 1991 and 1992.

Assume a ceding insurer enters into a contract in which its retention is a 75 percent loss ratio on a calendar basis on workers compensation business. In 1990, it has an 80 percent loss ratio so it will ultimately be reimbursed by its reinsurer for losses in excess of its 75 percent loss ratio retention. Reinsurance payments will probably not be received for several years because loss payments will be made by the ceding company until losses up to the 75 percent loss ratio retention are paid, but reinsurance payments will eventually be received. In 1991, it had a loss ratio of 70 percent, so all losses are within its retention and it will receive no reimbursement from its reinsurer.

Now assume the same ceding insurer (with the same premium volume and the same business reinsured) enters into a multi-year contract in which its retention is a 75 percent loss ratio over the two or more years term of the contract. In 1990, it has an 80 percent loss ratio and, in 1991, it has a 70 percent loss ratio. Thus, the ceding company's loss ratio over a two-year term is 75 percent and the ceding company will receive no reimbursement from the reinsurer. Hence, reimbursement to the ceding company is definitely delayed (in this example, forever), a violation of the necessary requirements to demonstrate transfer of risk.

Even if the loss ratio in 1991 was 75 percent, so that the resultant 1991-1992 two-year loss ratio was 77.5 percent, reimbursement of claims for 1990 could be delayed by the reinsurer for a year while waiting for 1991 loss ratio results.

[6] Assuming significant risk by the reinsurer means that the ceding insurer retains insignificant insurance risk on the reinsured portions. The term "insignificant" is defined in FAS 97 to mean "having little or no importance; trivial."

[7] The portion of any risk or obligation assumed by the reinsurer, when such portion is ascertained, shall be payable on demand of the ceding insurer at the same time as the ceding insurer shall pay its net retained portion of such risk or obligation, with reasonable provision for verification before payment, and the reinsurance shall be payable by the reinsurer, on the basis of the liability of the ceding insurer under the contract or contracts reinsured without diminution because of the insolvency of the ceding insurer. In the event of insolvency and the appointment of a conservator, liquidator or statutory successor of the ceding company, such portion shall be payable to such conservator, liquidator or statutory successor immediately upon demand, with reasonable provision for verification, on the basis of claims allowed against the insolvent company by any court of competent jurisdiction or by any conservator, liquidator, or statutory successor of the company having authority to allow such claims, without diminution because of such insolvency or because such conservator, liquidator or statutory successor has failed to pay all or a portion of any claims. Payments by the reinsurer as above set forth shall be made directly to the ceding insurer or to its conservator, liquidator or statutory successor, except where

the contract of insurance or reinsurance specifically provides another payee of such reinsurance in the event of the insolvency of the ceding insurer. (Extract from §922.2 California Insurance Code)

[8] *Ibid.*,p. 22-7

[9] *Ibid.*,p. 22-5

[10] The deposit may be reported as an admitted asset in the ceding company's annual statement (as a write-in item for "other than invested assets") if (1) the assuming company is licensed, accredited or otherwise qualified in the ceding company's state of domicile under Section 1 of the NAIC Model Law on Credit for Reinsurance or (b) there are funds held by or on behalf of the ceding company which meet the requirements of Section 2 of that law.

[11] *Ibid.*,p.22-7

[12] The other risk categories are asset risk — the risk of default of principal/interest or market value fluctuation; underwriting risk — the risk of underestimating liabilities on business already written or inadequately pricing business to be written; and off-balance sheet risk — risk associated with excessive growth, contingent liabilities and other non-balance sheet items.

[13] *NAIC Property/Casualty Risk-Based Capital Report*, Overview and Instructions, 12/31/94, p.12

[14] The loss and LAE risk is part of underwriting risk.

Exhibit 1:

Form 2

ANNUAL STATEMENT FOR THE YEAR 1992 OF THE .... (Name)

SCHEDULE F — PART 1A — SECTION 1

Ceded Reinsurance as of December 31, Current Year

NAIC Company Code	Federal ID Number	Name of Reinsurer*	Location**	†	1 Reinsurance Recoverable on Paid Losses and Paid Loss Adjustment Expenses, Days Overdue					2 Reinsurance Recoverable on Unpaid Losses and Unpaid Loss Adjustment Expenses***	3 Incurred But Not Reported (IBNR) Losses	4 Unearned Premiums (Estimated)	5 Reinsurance Premiums Ceded
					(a) Current 1-29	(b) 30-90	(c) 91-180	(d) Over 180	(e) Total				
059999	Totals												

*All companies should be listed in straight alphabetical order within the following groups with subtotals shown for each group; Affiliates; U.S. insurers and U.S. branches of alien insurers; pools, associations and similar underwriting facilities; and all other insurers.

**Show the precise location of the reinsurance company. For domestic insurers, report the city and state of the statutory home office. For alien insurers, report the city and country of domicile.

***Exclusive of Incurred But Not Reported included in Column 3.

†Insert in this column, if applicable, the following letter designation: (J) Reinsurer is subject to delinquency proceedings i.e. conservation, rehabilitation or liquidation, or in the case of an alien reinsurer, equivalent proceedings.

Exhibit 2:

Form 2

ANNUAL STATEMENT FOR THE YEAR 1993 OF THE ....
(Name)

SCHEDULE F — PART 3

Ceded Reinsurance as of December 31, Current Year (000 Omitted)

Federal ID Number	NAIC Company Code	Name of Reinsurer	Domiciliary Jurisdiction	1 Reinsurance Premiums Ceded	Reinsurance Recoverable On: 2 Paid Losses	3 Paid LAE	4 Known Case Loss Reserves	5 Known Case LAE Reserves	6 IBNR Loss Reserves	7 IBNR LAE Reserves	8 Unearned Premiums	9 Commissions (A)	10 Cols. 2 thru 9 Totals	Reinsurance Payable: 11 Ceded Balances Payable	12 Other Amounts Due to Reinsurers	13 Net Amount Recoverable From Reinsurance Col. 10-(11 + 12)	14 Funds Held By Company Under Reinsurance Treaties
9999999	Grand Totals																

(A) Report the five largest provisional commission rates included in the cedant's Reinsurance treaties. The commission rate to be reported is by contract with ceded premium in excess of $50,000.

	1 Name of Company	2 Commission Rate	3 Ceded Premium
1)			
2)			
3)			
4)			
5)			

Exhibit 3:

Form 2 **ANNUAL STATEMENT FOR THE YEAR 1993 OF THE** ....
(Name)

SCHEDULE F — PART 4
Aging of Ceded Reinsurance as of December 31, Current Year (000 Omitted)

Federal ID Number	NAIC Company Code	Name of Reinsurer	Domiciliary Jurisdiction	1 Current	Overdue 2 1 to 29 Days	3 30 — 90 Days	4 91 — 120 Days	5 Over 120 Days	6 Total Overdue Cols. 2 + 3 + 4 + 5	7 Total Due Cols. 1 + 6	8 Percentage Overdue Col. 6/Col. 7	9 Percentage more Than 120 Days Overdue Col. 5/Col. 7
9999999	Grand Totals											

Insurance and Reinsurance Terms

Most of the definitions listed below are taken from the glossary in the textbook, *Reinsurance*, edited by Robert W. Strain, CLU, CPCU, and published by Strain Publications, Wingdale, NY. Others are from *Reinsurance Contract Wording*, also edited by Robert W. Strain, and *Glossary of Insurance Terms,* edited by Thomas E. Green, CPCU, CLU; Robert W. Osler and John S. Bickley, Ph.D., published by The Merritt Company, Santa Monica, CA.

Acquisition Costs — The cost to an insurer of securing business, such as advertising, sales promotion and agent's and broker's commissions.

Admitted Assets — Assets recognized and accepted by state insurance laws in determining the solvency of insurers or reinsurers.

Admitted Company — (1) An insurer licensed to conduct business in a given state. (2) A reinsurer licensed or approved to conduct business in a given state.

Aggregate Excess-of-Loss Reinsurance — A form of excess-of-loss reinsurance which indemnifies the ceding company against the amount by which the ceding company's losses incurred during a specific period (usually 12 months) exceed either (1) a predetermined dollar amount or (2) a percentage of the company's base premiums for the specific period. This is commonly referred to as stop-loss reinsurance or excess-of-loss ratio reinsurance.

Alien Company — An insurance company organized under the laws of a foreign country.

Annual Statement — A summary of an insurance company's (or reinsurer's) financial operations for a particular year, including a balance sheet supported by detailed exhibits and schedules, filed with the state insurance department of each jurisdiction in which the company is licensed to conduct business. Also known as convention blank or convention statement.

Assume — To accept all or part of a ceding company's insurance or reinsurance on a risk or exposure.

Attachment Point — The amount at which excess reinsurance protection becomes operative; the retention under an excess reinsurance contract.

Authorized Reinsurance — Reinsurance placed with a reinsurer which is licensed or otherwise recognized by a particular state insurance department.

Base Premium — The ceding company's premiums (written or earned) to which the reinsurance premium rate is applied to produce the reinsurance premium.

Capacity — The measure of an insurer's financial strength to issue contracts of insurance, usually determined by the largest amount acceptable on a given risk or, in certain other situations, by the maximum volume of business it is prepared to accept.

Catastrophe — In insurance, a term applied for statistical recording purposes to an incident or series of related incidents involving an insured loss expected to exceed $5 million.

Catastrophe Reinsurance — A form of excess-of-loss reinsurance which, subject to a specific limit, indemnifies the ceding company against the amount of loss in excess of a specified retention. This loss amount represents the accumulation of losses resulting from a catastrophic event or series of events.

Cede — To transfer to a reinsurer all or part of the insurance or reinsurance written by a ceding company with the object of reducing the potential liability of the latter.

Ceding Commission — In reinsurance, an allowance (usually a percentage of the reinsurance premium) made by the reinsurer for part or all of a ceding company's acquisition and other costs. The ceding commission may also include a profit factor.

Ceding Company — An insurance company which cedes all or part of the insurance or reinsurance it has written to another insurer. A company that has placed reinsurance as distinguished from a company that accepts it. Also known as the reinsured.

Cession — The unit of insurance passed to a reinsurer by the primary company which issued a policy to the original insured. A cession accordingly may be the whole or a portion of single risks, defined policies or defined divisions of business, as agreed in the reinsurance contract.

Combined Ratio — The arithmetic sum of two ratios: incurred loss to earned premium, and incurred expense to written premium. Considered the best simple index to the current underwriting performance of an insurer. Also known as operating ratio.

Convention Statement — Another name for the annual statement form of National Association of Insurance Commissioners (NAIC). Also known as convention blank. The term "convention" is derived from the original name for the NAIC, which was the National Convention of Insurance Commissioners.

Direct Writer — (1) In reinsurance, a reinsurer which negotiates with a ceding company without benefit of an intermediary or broker. (2) In insurance, a primary insurer that sells insurance through licensed agents who produce business essentially for no one else.

Domestic Company — An insurer conducting business in its domiciliary state from which it received its charter to write insurance (as opposed to a foreign company: an insurer conducting business in a state other than its domiciliary state; or an alien company: one domiciled outside the United States but conducting business within the United States).

Earned Premium — The portion of a premium which is the property of an insurance company, based on the expired portion of the policy period.

Excess-of-Loss Ratio Reinsurance — See Aggregate Excess-of-Loss Reinsurance.

Excess-of-Loss Reinsurance — A generic term describing reinsurance which, subject to a specified limit, indemnifies the ceding company against all or a portion of the amount in excess of a specified retention.

Excess-per-Risk Reinsurance — A form of excess-of-loss reinsurance which, subject to a specified limit, indemnifies the ceding company against the amount of loss in excess of a specified retention with respect to each risk involved in each loss.

Exposure — The state of being subject to the possibility of loss; the extent of risk as measured by various standards such as payroll, gate receipts and area.

Facultative Reinsurance — The reinsurance of part or all of (the insurance provided by) a single policy in which each cession is negotiated separately. The primary company and the reinsurer have the option of accepting or declining each individual submission (as distinguished from the obligation to cede and accept to which the parties agree in treaty reinsurance).

Financial Reinsurance — See Finite Risk Reinsurance.

Finite Risk Reinsurance — A contract under which the ultimate liability of the reinsurer is capped (often by a maximum loss ratio) and on which anticipated investment income is expressly acknowledged as an underwriting component. Because this type of reinsurance is often purchased to ameliorate the balance sheet effects of statutory accounting principles, it is also known as Financial Reinsurance.

Foreign Company — An insurer conducting business in a state other than its domiciliary state.

Guaranty Fund — A fund, supported by assessments against solvent insurance companies, to absorb losses of claimants against insolvent insurers.

Incurred But Not Reported (IBNR) — The liability for future payments on losses which have already occurred but have not yet been reported in the reinsurer's records. This definition may be extended to include expected future development on claims already reported. See Loss Development.

Incurred Losses — (1) In insurance accounting, an amount representing the losses paid plus the change (positive or negative) in outstanding loss reserves within a given period of time. (2) Losses which have happened and which will result in a claim under the terms of an insurance policy or a reinsurance agreement.

Intermediary — A reinsurance broker who negotiates contracts of reinsurance on behalf of the reinsured, receiving a commission for placement and other services rendered.

Lead Reinsurer — The reinsurer recognized as the one of several reinsurers on a contract responsible for negotiating the initial terms of the contract.

Line — (1) Either the limit of insurance to be written which a company has fixed for itself on a class of risk (line limit), or the actual amount which it has accepted on a single risk or other unit. (2) A class or type of insurance (fire, marine or casualty, among others), also known as line of business. (3) The word "line" in reinsurance usually pertains to surplus reinsurance and means the amount of the reinsured's retention as respects each risk.

Lloyd's — Groups of individuals, called syndicates (not insurance companies), assuming liability through an underwriter. Each individual independently and personally assumes a proportionate part of the risk accepted by the underwriter. Generally refers to Lloyd's of London, England, where the Lloyd's Corporation provides the support facility for the group's activities.

Long-Tail Liability — A term used to describe certain types of third-party liability exposures (e.g., malpractice, products, errors and omissions) where the incidence of loss and the determination of damages are frequently subject to delays which extend beyond the term the insurance or reinsurance is in force. An example would be the contamination of a food product which occurs when the material is packed but which is not discovered until the product is consumed months or years later.

Loss Development — The difference between the estimated amount of loss as initially reported to the reinsurer and the estimated amount at a later date or the amount paid in final settlement.

Loss Ratio — Losses incurred expressed as a percentage of earned premiums.

Loss Reserve — For an individual loss, an estimate of the amount the insurer expects to pay for the reported claim. For total losses, estimates of expected payments for reported and unreported claims. May include amounts of loss adjustment expenses. See Incurred But Not Reported (IBNR) and Incurred Losses.

Loss Reserve Transfer — A type of reinsurance treaty through which companies can exchange certain types of liabilities. Also known as loss portfolio transfer.

Manager — In reinsurance, any person, partnership or corporation representing an insurer or reinsurer and underwriting for the insurer's or reinsurer's account.

Net Retention — The amount of insurance which an insurer keeps for its own account and does not reinsure in any way.

Nonadmitted Assets — Assets owned by an insurance company which are not recognized for solvency purposes by state insurance laws or insurance department regulations, e.g., premiums due and uncollected past 90 days, and furniture and fixtures, among others.

Nonadmitted Company — (1) An insurer not licensed in a given state. (2) A reinsurer not licensed or approved in a given state.

Nonadmitted Reinsurance — Reinsurance protection bought by a ceding company from a reinsurer not licensed or authorized to transact the particular line of business in the jurisdiction in question. No credit is given the ceding company for such nonadmitted reinsurance in its annual statement unless it withholds funds or holds a letter of credit on behalf of such unauthorized reinsurer.

Non-Proportional Reinsurance — Reinsurance under which the reinsurer's participation in a loss depends on the size of the loss. Also known as excess-of-loss reinsurance.

Occurrence — (1) An event that results in an insured loss. In some lines of insurance, such as liability, it is distinguished from an accident in that the loss does not have to be sudden and fortuitous. It can result from continuous or repeated exposure. (2) In reinsurance, per occurrence coverage permits all losses arising out of one event to be aggregated instead of being handled on a risk-by-risk basis.

Per Risk Reinsurance — Reinsurance in which the reinsurance limit and the retention apply "per risk" rather than per accident, per event, or in the aggregate.

Policyholders' Surplus — (1) The net worth of an insurer as reported in its annual statement. For a stock insurer, the sum of its surplus and capital. For a mutual insurer, its surplus. (2) The amount by which the assets of an insurer exceed the organization's liabilities. Another name for surplus to policyholders.

Pool — Any joint underwriting operation of insurance or reinsurance in which the participants assume a predetermined and fixed interest in all business written. Pools are often independently managed by professionals with expertise in the classes of business undertaken, and the members share equally in the premiums, losses, expenses and profits. An "association" and a "syndicate" (excluding that of Lloyd's of London) are both synonymous with a pool, and the basic principles of operation are much the same.

Portfolio Reinsurance — The transfer of a portfolio via a cession of reinsurance; the reinsurance of a run-off. Only policies in force (or losses outstanding) are reinsured, and no new or renewal business is included. Premium or loss portfolios, or both, may be reinsured. The term is sometimes applied to the reinsurance by one insurer of all business in force of another insurer retiring from an agency, a territory, or from the insurance business entirely.

Primary — An adjective applied in reinsurance to these nouns: insurer, insured, policy and insurance — meaning respectively: (1) the primary insurer is the insurance company which initially originates the business, i.e., the ceding company; (2) the primary insured is the policyholder insured by the primary insurer; (3) the primary policy is the initial policy issued by the primary insurer to the primary insured; (4) the primary insurance is the insurance covered under the primary policy issued (sometimes called "underlying insurance").

Professional Reinsurer — A term used to designate an organization whose business is mainly reinsurance and related services, as contrasted with other insurance organizations which may operate reinsurance-assuming departments in addition to their basic primary insurance business.

Pro Rata Reinsurance — A generic term describing all forms of reinsurance in which the reinsurer shares a proportional part of the original losses and premiums of the ceding company.
Also known as participating reinsurance and proportional reinsurance.

Quota-Share Reinsurance — A form of pro rata reinsurance (proportional) in which the reinsurer assumes an agreed percentage of each insurance being reinsured and shares all premiums and losses accordingly with the reinsured.

Rate — The percentage or factor applied to the ceding company's base premium to produce the reinsurance premium, or the percentage applied to the reinsurer's premium to produce the commission payable to the primary company (or, if applicable, the reinsurance intermediary).

Reciprocity — The mutual exchanging of reinsurance, often in equal amounts, from one party to another, the object of which is to stabilize overall results.

Reinsurance — The transaction whereby the reinsurer, for a consideration, agrees to indemnify the ceding company against all or part of the loss which the latter may sustain under the policy or policies which it has issued.

Reinsurance Commission — Another name for ceding commission.

Reinsurance Premium — An amount paid by the ceding company to the reinsurer in consideration for liability assumed by the reinsurer.

Reinsured — See Ceding Company.

Reinsurer — An organization which assumes the liability of another by way of reinsurance.

Retention — The amount which an insurer assumes for its own account. In pro rata contracts, the retention may be a percentage of the policy limit. In excess-of-loss contracts, the retention is a dollar amount of loss.

Retrocession — The transaction whereby a reinsurer cedes to another reinsurer all or part of the reinsurance it has previously assumed.

Risk — The chance of loss. Also used to refer to the insured or to property covered by a policy. In reinsurance, each company makes its own rules for defining units of hazard or single risks.

Social Inflation — The increasing of insurance losses caused by higher jury awards, more liberal treatment of claims by workers compensation boards, legislated rises in benefit levels (in some cases retroactively), and new concepts of tort and negligence, among others.

Stop-Loss Reinsurance — See Aggregate Excess-of-Loss Reinsurance.

Surplus-Share Reinsurance — A form of pro rata reinsurance indemnifying the ceding company against loss for the surplus liability ceded. Essentially, this can be viewed as a variable quota share contract wherein the reinsurer's pro rata share of insurance on individual risks will increase as the amount of insurance increases, in order that the primary company can limit its net exposure regardless of the amount of insurance written.

Surplus to Policyholders — (1) The net worth of an insurer as reported in its annual statement. For a stock insurer, the sum of its unassigned surplus and capital. (2) The amount by which the assets of an insurer exceed the organization's liabilities. Another name for policyholders' surplus.

Syndicate — An association of individuals or organizations organized to pursue certain insurance objectives. For example, individual underwriters in Lloyd's of London associate in separate syndicates to write marine insurance, reinsurance, life insurance, etc., entrusting the administrative details of each syndicate to a syndicate manager. See Pool.

Treaty — A reinsurance agreement between the ceding company and the reinsurer, usually for one year or longer, which stipulates the technical particulars applicable to the reinsurance of some class or classes of business.

Treaty Reinsurance — A standing agreement between reinsured and reinsurer for the cession and assumption of certain risks as defined in the treaty.

Umbrella Liability — A form of insurance protection against losses in excess of the amount covered by other liability insurance policies; also protects the insured in many situations not covered by the usual liability policies.

Unauthorized Insurer, Reinsurer — An insurer not licensed, or a reinsurer neither licensed nor approved, in a designated jurisdiction.

Unauthorized Reinsurance — Reinsurance placed with a reinsurer which does not have authorized status in the jurisdiction in question.

Underwriting Capacity — The maximum amount of money an insurer or reinsurer is willing to risk in a single loss event on a single risk or in a given period. The limit of capacity for an insurer or reinsurer may also be imposed by law or regulatory authority.

Unearned Premium Reserve — The sum of all the premiums representing the unexpired portions of the policies or contracts which the insurer or reinsurer has on its books as of a certain date. It is usually based on a formula of averages of issue dates and the length of term.

Write — To insure, to underwrite, or to accept an application for insurance.

Index

Additional Sources of Information

For additional information on reinsurance, please contact:

American Institute for Chartered Property Casualty Underwriters
P.O. Box 3020
720 Providence Road
Malvern, PA 19355-0770
Tel. 610-644-2100
Fax. 610-251-9995

Insurance Institute of America
P.O. Box 3016
720 Providence Road
Malvern, PA 19355-0716
Tel. 610-644-2101
Fax. 610-640-9576

Insurance Information Institute
110 William Street
New York, NY 10038-3901
Tel. 212-669-9200
Fax. 212-732-1916

Reinsurance Association of America
1301 Pennsylvania Avenue, NW
Suite 900
Washington, DC 20004-1701
Tel. 202-638-3690
Fax. 202-638-0936